ISLAMIC

ISIS, OIL AND ISRAEL

INFIDELS

#1 *NEW YORK TIMES* BESTSELLING AUTHOR

MIKE EVANS

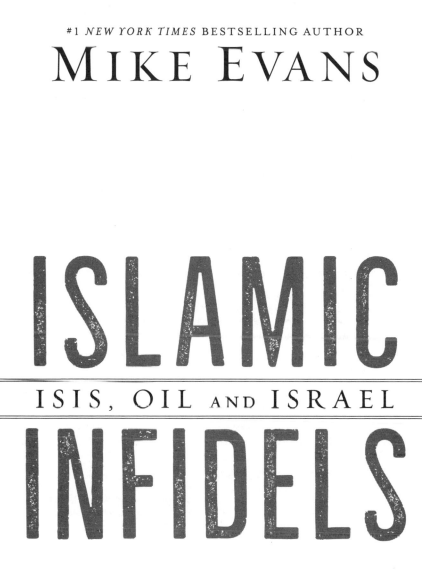

ISLAMIC

ISIS, OIL AND ISRAEL

INFIDELS

TimeWorthy
BOOKS

P.O. BOX 30000, PHOENIX, AZ 85046

The book is dedicated with
great admiration and appreciation to my friend
Andrew White,
vicar of St. George's Church in Baghdad.
It is the only Anglican church in the nation.
He pastored the congregation until he was forced
to depart in November 2014 due to security concerns.
He has been dubbed the "Vicar of Baghdad."

PREFACE

NO PRESIDENTIAL CANDIDATES debate should be complete without a lecture on radical Islam. The narrative is that if you are a liberal, you will not utter the phrase "radical Islam." It implies that America should be at war with radical Islam.

I am a proud American, but after forty years in the Middle East, I am convinced that playing the "radical Islam card" only benefits the jihadists. "Radical" to the Muslim world means "Salafi." "Salafi" (Arabic for ancestor) and "Islam" (submission) provide the entire basis for the Islamic religion and for Sharia Law—the Islamic legal system based on the Quran.

Saudi Arabia is the fertile ground in which radical Islam and ISIS—the Salafi militant group that subscribes to the Wahhabi doctrine of Sunni Islam—grows. The kingdom relies on its alliance with radical Islamic clergy which produces, legitimizes and defends Salafism. The West shakes the hand of Saudi officials while at the same time waging war with the Islamic State. Ninety-nine percent of all suicide bombers are Salafist Muslims. Salafism is the purest form of radical religion.

To declare war on radical Islam is to declare war on all Islam, since sixty percent of Muslims are fundamentalist, radical Salafists—no less than 750 million people. It's exactly what jihadists want. It is much more accurate to define all jihadists as "Islamic infidels" and control the terms of the terror ideological war. ISIS should be renamed ISI—Islamic State Infidels.

If we are going to war against radical Islam, we need to include the countries of Turkey, Indonesia, Saudi Arabia, Kuwait, Iraq, Lebanon, Jordan, Egypt and at least a dozen others. If we really believed that armed conflict is needed to stem the tide of fundamentalism, then why did we go to war to save Kuwait, a radical Islamic Salafist state? Or fight one of America's longest wars ever in Iraq, another radical Islamic state? The answers to those questions are numerous and complicated.

The U.S. knows how to defeat ISIS, but it will require the same search strategy that was utilized to defeat al Qaeda. The problem now is that this strategy does not have the support of the American people or Sunni tribesmen. As we will see later, it was from this corrupt Iraqi Shiite, pro-Iran government that the virus which is ISIS sprang and grew into the feared terrorist organization it has become.

After the protracted war in Iraq, there is no desire to go back into that quagmire and sacrifice more American lives. The total number of U.S. troops killed in combat in Iraq was 4,487, with 32,223 wounded, and ISIS knows this. How, then, does the U.S. defeat ISIS? America must fight an ideological war—ground zero in defeating ISIS. In order for ISIS to grow it will require a war with the "Great Satan," America and the "Small Satan," Israel.

Traditional warfare is like killing flies. The director of Israeli intelligence and my friend, the late Isser Harel, said to me, "You kill a fly in America and rejoice. We kill one in the Middle East and one hundred come to the funeral." The traditional wars of the twentieth century are obsolete. Twenty-first century conflicts have become ideological, economic, media-driven, proxy wars. Unless or until America wins the ideological war, the cancer will continue to mutate.

I asked the late Prime Minister Ariel Sharon to tell me how many Arab Christians blow themselves up attempting to kill Jews. His response was, "None; why?"

I made that point because not all Arabs want to blow themselves up; the vast majority of Muslims are not jihadists. Yes, some may be radical, but they don't want self-destruction. In the Muslim world, calling someone honorable is the highest compliment and to cause them humiliation is worse than death. Do we really want to declare war on radical Islam and 750 million Muslims?

Do we really think we can humiliate them into submission? That method alone will not defeat radical Islam if we paint the target with such a broad brush. We must analyze what other options might be more effective. In that study, there are several questions that come to mind: Why must a terrorist's name be acknowledged? Why not simply place an "X" or label them "she" or "he" instead of using a name? Why must a terrorist even be acknowledged as a radical Islamic jihadist? Would it motivate them if the words used to describe them were, "Islamic Infidels?" If the jihadists are at war with the infidels, do you think they want to be labeled as one, as well?

A jihadist should not be lionized; but must instead be demonized. Refusing to acknowledge who they are, but only calling the individual an "Islamic infidel" accomplishes that objective.

Since 9/11, America has focused on who kills us, but not

on why they kill. The answer is always the same: Jihadists believe we are infidels. We must turn the Islamic infidel card back on them, and we must persuade the Muslim world to join us, especially since the majority of those whom jihadists kill are Muslim. How about taking a few billion dollars we use on bombs and blanket the internet with an "Islamic infidel" campaign?

Secondly, we must employ Israel as a strategic proxy. Israel helped America win the cold war in the Middle East without the U.S. sacrificing lives. When President Harry S Truman recognized the reborn State of Israel in 1948, his decision reflected the possibility of Soviet advancement into that region of the Middle East. Christian Science Monitor contributor Joseph Harsch, in a radio address, told his audience that "losing Palestine would mean Russia could 'strangle American interests not only in the Mediterranean but throughout the Western world'. Even Congressional leaders were reported to be 'now concerned' that 'the Cold War is expanding into the Middle East.".[1]

Once again, Israel can assist the U.S. by helping to defeat ISIS—and we need Israel to do just that. The Jewish state cannot be of assistance if she is weakened.

Jurgen Todenhofer, a former member of the German

parliament, spent time with ISIS fighters behind enemy lines. He related to the *Jewish News* that

> The only country ISIS fears is Israel. They told me they know the Israeli army is too strong for them . . . they know the Israelis are very tough as far as fighting against guerrillas and terrorists . . . . They are not scared of the British and the Americans, they are scared of the Israelis . . . the Israeli army is the real danger . . . . These people [the IDF] can fight a guerrilla war.[2]

Thirdly, the U.S. must fight a special ops war. You cannot bomb ISIS into oblivion, especially since it is able to use the bombing videos of civilians being killed to recruit ten times more jihadists than are eliminated. In the Islamic video business, America is perceived as a Goliath to their David. That perception must no longer be allowed to take root. Al Qaeda mutated into ISIS. It, too, will mutate into another terror regime if the deadly virus is not destroyed.

Fourthly, Islamic infidels must be bankrupted. When

the Islamic state of Iran receives $150 billion compliments of the U.S., America is not serious about defeating Islamic infidels. ISIS will not go away any time soon. It can be defeated, but not without an ideological war that demonizes ISIS and all jihadists as Islamic infidels.

1

THE BEGINNING:
ISIS AND OIL

*ISIS's urgent goal is not to affect the commodity markets,
but to fill its own coffers. Then again, its bigger goal is
to scare the whole world. Now, ISIS's failure to instill
in the oil markets the kind of fears it has instilled
elsewhere, can be counted as its first strategic defeat.*[3]

AMOTZ ASA-EL,
COLUMNIST

BEFORE THE IRAQ WAR BEGAN, I wrote *Beyond Iraq:
The Next Move.* In the pages of that book, I predicted what
would happen in Iraq in a battle between the Shia and Sunni
Muslims. As a result of that book, in 2007 I was invited by
President Mahmoud Barzani of Kurdistan for a state visit.
While there, I met with the president, his Minister of the
Interior, speaker of the Kurdish government, the head of the

Kurdistan equivalent of the FBI, the Minister of State, the vice president, and members of the Kurdish government.

During those meetings, I was made aware that something existential was transpiring in Iraq. I wrote a sequel to my first book and titled it, *The Final Move Beyond Iraq, The Final Solution While the World Sleeps*. On the back cover, I stated, "An Islamic revolution is spreading and is on the brink of becoming America's greatest threat since the [American] Civil War."

The book, a #1 *New York Times* bestseller, predicted the birth of an Islamic Sunni caliphate. Derived from the word "caliph", a caliphate is the area controlled by what is historically considered to be a successor to Mohammad. The caliph is the political leader of the area and head of the Islamic nation. The establishment of such a caliphate is drawing ever closer with the rise of the Islamic State— or as it has become known in its many mutations: ISIS, IS, or ISIL. The battle is one between authoritarianism and any move toward democracy. Some Middle East countries are now losing the battle either because of low oil revenues or a complete loss of that income. CIA Director John Brennan said in January 2016 that an ISIS attack on the United States was "inevitable." According to Brennan:

We have a number of instances where ISIL has used chemical munitions on the battlefield. There are reports that ISIS has access to chemical precursors and munitions that they can use.[4]

Reports of mustard gas in the hands of ISIS began in the summer of 2015. Kurdish troops in Syria related exposure to the chemical during a confrontation with Islamic State terrorists.

ISIS has commandeered millions of dollars in revenue, i.e., banks, oil, gas reserves, taxation, extortion, kidnapping, and donations from some Gulf Oil States under the guise of humanitarianism. It is using every conceivable social network from Twitter, Friendica, Diasporamessenger.com, and Quitter to spread its message in more than twenty-three languages. Recruits are joining from Tunisia, Saudi Arabia, Russia, Jordan, Morocco, France, Turkey, Lebanon, Germany, Libya, the United Kingdom, Indonesia, Uzbekistan, Pakistan, virtually the known world, and sadly, the United States.

It may seem more like fiction than reality, but the truth is: ISIS controls portions of Iraq and Syria, an area with a population of eight million. The lives of the inhabitants under its control are a living hell. According to Bernard Haykel, a professor of Near-Eastern Studies at Princeton:

> Slavery, crucifixion, and beheadings are not something that freakish [jihadists] are cherry-picking from the medieval tradition. [They are] bringing it wholesale into the present day.[5]

There are few news reports about the spread of ISIS into Algeria, Yemen, West Africa, the northern provinces of Southeast Asia, and the enormous impact on Libya, Egypt, Afghanistan, Nigeria, and even the threat to Israel. ISIS claims religious and military authority over the entire Muslim world. It is also well-versed on how to integrate into the Middle East and the West quietly and carefully, preparing for an eventual overthrow.

ISIS leaders refer to their strongholds as *Dar al-Islam*—the house of Islam. Not only are a large number of al-Qaeda defectors involved, but also military leaders and members of the late Saddam Hussein's Ba'ath Party. Disenfranchised, unemployed masses raised on the precepts of Islam are inspired by dreams of an Islamic caliphate, and the belief that it can conquer the world.

This is partially because it is an authoritarian regime, an entity similar to the government in Saudi Arabia that dumbs-down the masses for its own benefit.

What ISIS believes about prophecy has a sense of plausibility: that when the end of time arrives, not only will it take over the world, but that Jesus, who is considered a prophet in Islam, will return to earth and join them. He will help lead the Muslims to victory against Jews, Christians and the Antichrist—the deceiver who claims to be the Christian Messiah. This teaching is a huge selling-point in recruiting foreign jihadists to join what IS heralds as the final battle of the Apocalypse.

It will be the battle between the modern-day Crusader armies and Islam. This is one reason ISIS needs—and wants—such a battle between the Muslims and the United States of America. Its leaders believe it will legitimize their cause and help recruit additional members. This feeds the group's desire to do everything possible to provoke the U.S. into a fight. They believe ISIS is a legitimate caliphate with Abu Bakr al-Baghdadi as its caliph.

The caliphate called "ISIS" is not only a threat in the Middle East, but is an extremely serious problem worldwide. Author David Ignatius wrote of its threat:

ISIS is mysterious in part because it is so many things at once. It combines Islamic piety and reverence for the prophet and his companions with the most modern social-media platforms and encryption schemes; its videos blend the raw pornographic violence of a snuff film with the pious chanting of religious warriors; the group has the discipline of a prison gang (many of its recruits were indeed drawn from U.S.-organized prisons in Iraq), but also the tactical subtlety and capacity for deception of the most skilled members of Saddam Hussein's intelligence services, who were also pulled into the ISIS net. It appears less brittle than al-Qaeda because its members care less about religious doctrine and organizational hierarchy.[6]

Not only are Crusaders targeted, ISIS terrorists readily behead Muslims as was the case with 15-year old Ayham Hussein. He was caught in Mosul, Iraq by a faithful ISIS follower and held captive by other members of the death cult. According to an article in the *Jerusalem Post*, Ayham was hauled before a sharia court, beaten and judged guilty. He was then dragged into the town square and beheaded. His crime: listening to Western music. No one—Muslim or Christian, Jew or gentile—is safe from the barbarism of ISIS.

The Middle East is on the brink of an Islamic explosion. The hopes ignited by an Islamic/Sunni caliphate are mesmerizing to the youth of the Muslim world. A global coalition attempting to defeat ISIS is failing. The terrorist group is spreading through the world's blood stream like a terminal cancer. Jihadist groups in thirty countries have pledged allegiance to or support for ISIS, i.e., Boko Haram in Nigeria and Velayat Sinai in Egypt. Reports from Turkey indicate that even intelligence officials with the government of President Recep Tayyip Erdoğan have found a way to turn a blind eye to ISIS infiltrators wishing to cross the border to support the terrorist group. This collaboration is similar to that which took place between Osama bin Laden and the Pakistani intelligence service which also turned a blind eye to the al Qaeda leader living in their midst.

In later chapters of this book, you will see how the birth process for ISIS has created and unleashed a Frankenstein-type monster. Its architects have totally lost control of the beast. Gulf State corporations, loosely called "countries", have employed oil-produced revenues to pay off Islamic fundamentalists, while extorting more moderate Muslims in an attempt to keep the ogre at bay. ISIS claims that all emirate groups, states, and organizations are illegitimate, while it desires to conquer the world and usher in the final battle of the Apocalypse.

ISIS has ties to Wahhabism which was birthed in Saudi Arabia and continues to flourish there. This branch of Islam began in the eighteenth century when cleric and academic Muhammad ibn Abd al-Wahhab fostered a revival of ultra-conservative, pure Islam. His doctrine is echoed in the ISIS appeal for the purification of Islam. It considers all other branches of Islam to be apostate. No other Islamic movement has emphasized apocalyptism—the idea that civilization will soon come to a tumultuous end due to some sort of catastrophic global event.[7] This sect also believes that the arrival of the one known as the Mahdi is near.

The name given to the sect, Twelvers, is derived from twelve supposedly divinely ordained leaders—

imams—descendants of Mohammad. At the age of five, the Mahdi, the last of the twelve, was supposedly hidden from view in a state often referred to as "occultation." In the midst of turmoil and warfare, it is believed the last imam will be revealed and will establish a worldwide caliphate with Shia Islam at its center.

Of great significance to the ISIS hordes is the large Syrian village of Dabiq. The Islamic State is so focused on the prophecy regarding Dabiq that it has given that name to its stylish, glossy, and artistically designed magazine. To maximize its reach, the publication is translated into a number of languages including English.

Journalist Anna Glanville wrote an article for British newspaper, *The Guardian,* which clarifies the prophecy:

> The 1,300-year-old hadith, which is a report of the deeds, teachings and sayings of the Prophet Mohammed, refers to the 'horde' flying 80 banners as they take on a Muslim army in the Syrian town of Dabiq . . . . Supporters appear to be convinced of the prophecy's validity, with one writing on Twitter: "Dabiq will happen for

certain. The U.S. and its allies will descend on Syria once they see that the air campaign has failed. That is a promise by God and his Messenger."

Another, from Tunisia, wrote. "The lions of Islam have raised the banner of the Caliphate in Dabiq. Now they await the arrival of the Crusader army."[8]

In a threatening ISIS rant released in September 2014, its spokesman exposited:

> And so we promise you by Allah's permission that this campaign will be your final campaign. It will be broken and defeated, just as all your previous campaigns were broken and defeated, except that this time we will raid you thereafter, and you will never raid us. We will conquer your Rome, break your crosses, and enslave your women, by the permission of Allah, the Exalted.[9]

No matter how the lines are drawn, ISIS depends on oil revenue to fund its extremism. Recent events in Syria and Northern Iraq have revealed the correlation between oil and power and how vulnerable the Islamic State is when its funds dry up. The Islamic State has established its own financial composition based on its control of oil-fields in that area. The fields in question are the al-Tamak and al-Omar in Syria and the Qayyara field near Mosul. ISIS built revenues based on illegally selling oil to fund its organization in the amount of approximately $40 million per month. Coalition members have made inroads with bombing runs that target production and refining facilities controlled by ISIS.

In late 2015 journalist Nick Butler summarized information from the *Iraq Oil Report* giving a glimpse of how the Islamic State has been hampered by the attacks:

> Production is down as field infrastructure has been hit by bombing. Some oil continues to flow automatically and has to be stored temporarily in holes dug hurriedly in the ground.
>
> Key refining links have been broken forcing the use of primitive techniques using open pits to make usable products.

The fall in the price has cut margins—already low because of discounting and is discouraging the black market trade because the risks involved now far outstrip the rewards especially for the tanker drivers.[10]

A recent Fox News article contends that:

The extremists who once bragged about minting their own currency are having a hard time meeting expenses, thanks to coalition airstrikes and other measures that have eroded millions from their finances since last fall. Having built up loyalty among militants with good salaries and honeymoon and baby bonuses, the group has stopped providing even the smaller perks: free energy drinks and Snickers bars . . . . An exile from al-Bab said low-level fighters there have begun to grumble, and townspeople have overheard Islamic State officials discussing crippling airstrikes on oil infrastructure in

Syria and Iraq and the cutoff of supply
lines and revenue sources.[11]

Even the debilitating strikes against ISIS in Syria and Iraq are by no means indicative of its lack of oil revenue opportunities. There are major fields awaiting an assault by the terrorist group in Libya, Algeria and in Egypt. And it has not given up on capturing other Iraq oil facilities near Kirkuk and Mosul.

Unlike the Iraqi oilfields, the Saudi Arabia fields may not be in the crosshairs of ISIS as yet; they are thought to be too highly-patrolled and too tightly-controlled. However, with its ties to Wahhabism and the late Osama bin Laden, who knows what the future will bring between the Saudi kingdom and the ISIS caliphate.

Current political conditions in the post-Arab Spring climate, and especially in hypocritical, oil-rich, family-owned corporations called countries only feeds and fuels the narrative in the minds of unemployed, impoverished youth. In the past, countries such as Saudi Arabia could export terror and use social welfare and bribery to trivialize the rhetoric being taught in mosques and madrassas by the mullahs. Now, thanks to the oil crisis, those dollars have disappeared.

The solution is for the Western world to castigate ISIS

as Islamic Infidels. They must be branded with that name that identifies outcasts of the Islamic faith. The cancer of ISIS will metastasize, feeding on global oil to nurture and ultimately change the balance of the contest in the Middle East.

2

ISLAMIC INFIDELS: THE DEFINITION

"Islam is a religion of peace, one which is compatible with respect for human rights and peaceful coexistence."

POPE FRANCIS, DECEMBER 25, 2014

SINCE SEPTEMBER 11, 2001, the question most asked about Islam is this: Is Islam a peaceful religion as some have said, and if so, why are there repeated calls to slay infidels? This leads to my next question: Who are the infidels? Are they only Christians? Only Jews? Or does that call also include Islamic Infidels—those who have prostituted the "peaceful Islamic religion?"

"Infidel" is defined as: a pejorative [or derogatory] term used in certain religions for those who do not believe the central tenets of one's own religion.[12] By this definition, those Islamists who do not adhere to the interpretation that Islam is peaceful and choose to shun that part of the Quran could readily be labeled Islamic Infidels.

Choices are made daily by U.S. leaders, the consequences of which will last our lifetime, and perhaps beyond. It is imperative that decisions be made regarding the onslaught of terrorism perpetrated by Islamic Infidels. This book explores how that might be accomplished.

On December 17, 2001, approximately two months following the attacks on New York City and Washington and on the airliner that was downed in a field in Pennsylvania, President George W. Bush visited the Islamic Center of Washington, D.C. In his speech, he stated:

> The English translation is not as eloquent as the original Arabic, but let me quote from the Koran, itself: In the long run, evil in the extreme will be the end of those who do evil. For that they rejected the signs of Allah and held them up to ridicule.
>
> The face of terror is not the true faith of Islam. That's not what Islam is all about. Islam is peace. These

terrorists don't represent peace. They represent evil and war.[13]

First, we must examine the verse in the Quran that advocates the slaughter of infidels. It is found in Surah 9:5:

> But when the sacred months are passed away, kill the idolaters (non-Muslims) wherever ye may find them; and take them, and besiege them, and lie in wait for them in every place of observation.

According to Sahar Aziz, associate professor at Texas A&M School of Law, Middle Eastern "thugocracies" are to blame for much of the role of terrorism in today's society. She writes:

> With a few exceptions, Muslim-majority countries are ruled by undemocratic monarchies, military leaders, or secular dictators . . . . Elections are either outright rigged or manipulated through abuse of law to guarantee the rulers' stay in power . . . . The less fortunate dissidents are tried before

military courts or victims of extrajudi-
cial killings. And a small minority joins
terrorist groups to respond to state violence with their own violence . . . . Each
government has its own official imam
to issue fatwas to grant the regime religious legitimacy. Verses and Islamic
doctrines mandating obedience to
the ruler are emphasized. Mosques,
Islamic universities and other religious
institutions are controlled by the state
to ensure their lectures and curricu-
lums do not threaten the regime's grip
on power . . . . Terrorist groups mir-
ror the state's exploitation of religion.
Rather than call for obedience of the
state, they selectively cite Islamic texts
to mobilize Muslims to fight against
oppression. Terrorists cloak their political agenda—to overthrow regimes—in
religious rhetoric.[14]

Islamic State terrorists are quick to explain that their
core motivation is, indeed, the religion of the Muslim

faithful; that they are driven by devotion to Allah and the Quran. This is why their every act of violence is prefaced with "Alluha Akbar"—God is greater. Muslim Brotherhood founder, Hassan al-Banna, expounded on jihad and Islam when he wrote: "It is the nature of Islam to dominate, not to be dominated, to impose its law on all nations and to extend its power to the entire planet."[15]

If religion is not then at the center of jihadism, what is? I believe, succinctly stated, "It is power." In the seventh century, as the Arab hoards began to make their way northward, Christians were forced to convert to Islam, pay the jizya, (tax/ tribute), or die by the sword. In 570 AD an event took place that would forever change the entire world: The Prophet Mohammad was born. The rise of Islam—the religion founded by Muhammad ibn Abdullah, regarded in the Muslim world as a messenger and prophet of God, resulted in nations being conquered by nomads armed with a totally different weapon—a new religion. People welcomed new leadership and embraced Islam's five pillars of faith: 1) "There is no god but Allah, and Mohammad is the Prophet of Allah; 2) Prayer (to always be in touch with God); 3) Pilgrimage to Mecca; 4) Fasting in order to feel the pain of the disadvantaged and to develop self-discipline; and 5) Alms or charitable contributions."[16]

The invading armies were ruthless—coldblooded and dedicated to conquest. Boasting of their piousness, the Saracens—the word used to designate Muslims before the sixteenth century—were said to be both fervent in faith and ferocious in conquest. Guided by Mohammad's religious dogma, the Saracen quest was one of domination whatever the cost to those subjugated.

To view today's Islamic State infidels is to look back in time to the Saracens and their brutal brand of Islam. They adhere slavishly to their interpretation of the Quran and the Sunnah, or Mohammad's edicts verbally transmitted from one to another. The harshest verses are used to nullify the more humane treatment of non-Muslims. This proselytizing of the Quran by Islamic Infidels serves only to ignite the fires of jihad. The hatred does not stop with Christians and Jews—declared to be infidels by the Islamic State—but also to other Muslims who have been captured. Resorting to the practice called *takfir*, the imprisoned Islamists are first declared to be *kafir*—or unbelievers—so they, too, can be subjected to imprisonment, slavery or even beheading.

The dilemma is that radical Islamic Infidels are the diametric opposite of Christians whose central belief is love—for God and for fellowman. The centrality of radical Islam is that of power, not peace. The mandate for followers of IS revolves around total submission and unmitigated fear. The double standard practiced by IS and its Islamic Infidels was the subject of an article by *Associated Press* journalist Hamza Hendawi:

> Mohammed Saad, a Syrian activist, was imprisoned by the Islamic State group, hung by his arms and beaten regularly. Then one day, his jailers quickly pulled him and other prisoners down and hid them in a bathroom.
>
> The reason? A senior Muslim cleric was visiting to inspect the facility. The cleric had told the fighters running the prison that they shouldn't torture prisoners and that anyone held without charge must be released within 30 days, Saad told The Associated Press. Once the coast was clear,

the prisoners were returned to their torment.

"It's a criminal gang pretending to be a state," Saad said, speaking in Turkey, where he fled in October [2015]. "All this talk about applying Shariah and Islamic values is just propaganda, Daesh is about torture and killing," he said, using the Arabic acronym for IS.

Syrians who have recently escaped the Islamic State group's rule say public disillusionment is growing as IS has failed to live up to its promises to install a utopian "Islamic" rule of justice, equality and good governance.[17]

Daesh—a new acronym for the blood-thirsty Islamic State—is in Arabic: Al-Dawla al-Islamiya fi al-Iraq wa al-Sham. This roughly translates as "To trample down and crush" or "a bigot who imposes his view on others." French Foreign Minister Laurent

Fabius was among the first to adopt this insulting slang term:

> This is a terrorist group and not a state. I do not recommend using the term Islamic State because it blurs the lines between Islam, Muslims and Islamists. The Arabs call it Daesh and I will be calling them the "Daesh cutthroats." [18]

Many IS followers are faced with making the decision of whom to serve. In the Bible, Joshua assumed the mantle of leadership from Moses and led the Children of Israel into the Promised Land. When Joshua had completed the tasks God had assigned him, he called the people together and charged them with the most important decision of their lives. In Joshua 24:15, NKJV, the challenge is issued:

> And if it seems evil to you to serve the LORD, choose for yourselves this day whom you will serve, whether the gods which your fathers served that *were* on the other side of the River, or the gods of the Amorites, in whose

land you dwell. But as for me and my
house, we will serve the LORD.

Singer/songwriter Bob Dylan in his song, "Gotta
Serve Some-body," wrote:

> But you're gonna have to serve somebody, yes
> Indeed you're gonna have to serve somebody
> Well, it may be the devil or it may be the Lord
> But you're gonna have to serve somebody.[19]

Islamic Infidels have made the choice to serve Satan,
to take the path of murder and mayhem, to kill, steal and
destroy—the way of Satan, not the way of peace. Rather
than name names or attach labels—IS, Hezbollah, Hamas,
Fatah, or other of the myriad of terrorist organizations—
why not just leave these jihadists in obscurity and simply
call them Islamic Infidels?

The first mention of this appellation to be found on
the Internet was an article I submitted to the *Jerusalem
Post* in late 2015. It read, in part:

> Since 9/11, America has focused on
> who kills us, but not on why they kill.
> The answer is always the same: They
> believe we are infidels . . . . We must

play the Islamic infidel card on them, and we must persuade the Muslim world to join us, especially since the majority of those whom jihadists kill are Muslim.[20]

Only time will reveal if this proposed tactic is successful.

3

SALAFISM AND
WAHHIBISM

---

*Militant Salafis place great emphasis on
jihad, which they interpret as armed struggle
and regard as a religious duty.*[21]

AFTER FORTY YEARS of having worked in the Middle East, I am convinced that playing the "war against radical Islam card" only benefits the jihadists. As I have indicated, the word "radical" in the Muslim world is equated with *Salafi*, a term used to describe "Fundamental Islamic thought."

Saudi Arabia relies on its alliance with radical Islamic clergy that produces, legitimizes and defends Salafism. Sadly, the majority of suicide bombers tend to be Salafist Muslims.

Salafism provides the entire basis for Sharia Law in the Muslim religion and is the purest form of radical religion which goes to the root of Salafism. Dr. Ghayas Saddiqui of the Muslim Parliament of Great Britain relates:

There is no moderation in [the Salafis] approach . . . . It is a very strict interpretation of Islam, and their attitude to both non-Muslims and Muslims who are not with them is very harsh."[22]

According to Muhammad Munir, assistant professor of law at the International Islamic University in Islamabad, Pakistan, suicide attacks may, in fact, breach a number of Islamic laws:

Under Islamic *jus in bello* [international humanitarian law] perfidy or treachery is prohibited, the intentional killing or targeting of women, children and other civilians is strictly banned, the principle of reciprocity is not applicable when it would entail acts that are prohibited in Islam, and the destruction of civilian objects and property is not allowed. Under Islamic law "martyrdom" attacks are allowed only if the following conditions are met:

✦ They may only take place during a war;

✦ They must be carried out by soldiers;

✦ The soldiers must not pretend to be non-combatants;

✦ The attacks must not harm civilians or civilian property; and,

✦ The device used must not mutilate bodies.

When a suicide bomber targets civilians, he might be committing at least five crimes according to Islamic law, namely killing civilians, mutilating them by blowing them up, violating the trust of the enemy's soldiers and civilians, committing suicide and, finally, destroying civilian objects or property. In my opinion, because of

the crimes committed he—or she—is
not a shaheed (martyr).

Those who call such a person "shaheed" are simply ignoring the teachings of the Qur'an and the Sunnah
with regard to the Islamic *jus in bello*
[Latin term for "law of war"] and are
making a mockery of God's law.[23]

If the Salafis are the largest singular group practicing
suicide bombings, can they not then be labeled Islamic
Infidels because they are in opposition to traditional
Islam?

In 1991, Ayman al-Zawahiri, second only to Osama bin
Laden in the al Qaeda hierarchy, penned a leaflet, *Bitter
Harvest*. In the text, he challenged Muslims to return to
the true faith and leaders to rule only according to the
laws of Allah. Those who were deemed to be corrupt and
who refused to step down were to be removed from their
lofty positions by means of jihad. Zawahiri challenges
democracy as a religion and avows its downfall by means
of jihad.[24]

This faction composed of religious Salafis strikes fear
in the hearts of those who desire true democracy in the

Middle East. Salafists are members of an ultra-fundamen-talist sect of Sunni Islam which controls the majority in the Kingdom of Saudi Arabia. The group strongly supports the establishment of a caliphate and is described as doc-trinally rigid. The fundamentalist teachings of Salafism do have close ties to Wahhabism, an extremely anti-Shiite group in the Kingdom.

What are the basic differences between Wahhabism and Salafism? The Wahhabis support a strict system of Sunni Islam with the emphasis on an authoritarian view of sharia law. It boasts an exact interpretation of Mohammad's writings. The Wahhabi faction was estab-lished in the eighteenth century by Mohammed ibn al-Wahhab, a scholar from Najd. Their beliefs are closely related to those espoused by the Taliban. Perhaps it is because of this that Wahhabism is often said to be a significant source for global terrorism. During a Senate Sub-committee hearing on terrorism, Senator Jon Kyl of Arizona stated:

> The extreme nature of Wahhabism
> is well established. As the great
> scholar of Islam, Bernard Lewis, has
> noted, "Saudi oil revenues have,"

and I am quoting here, "allowed the Saudis to spread this fanatical, destructive form of Islam all over the Muslim World and among the Muslims in the West. Without oil and the creation of the Saudi kingdom, Wahhabism would have remained a lunatic fringe."[25]

It is also thought to be Wahhabism that has motivated IS, sometimes known as ISIL, the Islamic State of Iraq and the Levant, and has bred disharmony among the Islamic sects. Muslims who fail to agree with the Wahhabists have often been summarily executed for apostasy. Historical monuments and crypts have been smashed and artifacts scattered—not only those of other faiths, but of the Muslim religion as well. Alexander H. Joffe, a writer for the Middle East Forum website, offered the following about of the Islamic State's total disregard for antiquities:

Two explanations have been offered. This first is Islamic antipathy towards the pre-Islamic past. The second is that the group profits from selling looted antiquities. But there is a third and equally sinister reason that has barely been mentioned. Both destruction and looting comprise a system of social control over captive populations, a system that strives to regulate individual behavior down to the level of digging holes in the ground.[26]

The words "Wahhabi" and "Salafi" were often substituted one for the other as the two groups began to merge in the 1960s. Steve Coll wrote in his column in *The New Yorker*:

> Some Saudis acknowledge their country's dominant theology as a distinct school of Islamic thought, but they will typically refer to this school as Salafism, a term that refers to the beliefs and practices of the earliest followers of Islam. With some exceptions, adherents of the Salafi school steer away from purposeful political organizing; instead, they often emphasize matters of personal

faith, such as the strict regulation of Islamic rituals, and of an individual's private conduct and prayer. Bin Laden's group . . . was influenced to some extent by Salafi ideas, because there was no escaping the presence of such ideas in Saudi society, but bin Laden's group adopted "a more activist or a political agenda," . . . drawn largely from the Muslim Brotherhood's advocacy for political change in Islamic countries.[27]

Within Wahhabism, one is required to observe and practice the laws and doctrines of Islam. Respect and admiration for anyone, past or present, is seen as apostasy and is punishable by no less than death. Prejudice, sexism and bigotry are the order of the day. Adherents are warned to shun infidels—and all who do not follow Wahhabism are classified as unbelievers. Those who fail to follow the tenets of Wahhabism will eventually be subjected to punishment in a burning hell.

A contributor to the website Scholars and Rogues, wrote of the ties between terrorism and religion:

There's a very obvious reason why it could be the religion itself which is the cause of terror: It's a religion with a set of beliefs fundamentally at odds with those that underpin our modern society.

Consider free speech . . . . The leaders of virtually every Islamic country, from Iran to Egypt to Saudi to Turkey, have instituted severe restrictions on the press.

Or consider women's rights and education. Boko Haram, the popular name of the Nigerian-based Islamic terrorist group that raided a girls school and kidnapped 276 girls consigning them to slavery, actually means "education is forbidden." . . . Even in those Muslim countries where women are not killed for the crime of education, they're still controlled and limited in everything from dress to driving a car . . . .

Keep going down the list—

democratically elected governments, freedom to worship, independent judiciaries, tolerance of minorities, etc. It's a long list, and Islam is at odds with most of it . . . . **the problem isn't just that radical Islamists have adopted a set of violent tactics that we abhor, but rather that the belief system itself just doesn't fit in a modern world** . . . . Our devotion to religious tolerance and democracy doesn't really work so well when dealing with a religion that doesn't believe in either tolerance or democracy . . . .

If a Christian criticizes Islam, for example, it's seen as self-serving. Well, I'm an atheist . . . . And it's because I'm an atheist that I object to letting Islam off the hook for terror. Islamic terrorists aren't attacking churches, they're attacking schools and newspapers.[28] (Emphasis in original text.)

As if Wahhabism weren't enough with which to contend, Salafism too, emphasizes a true and genuine brand of Islam with a return to an earlier Muslim lifestyle—no modern-day conveniences or dress. Journalist Mansour al-Nogaidan in an article for the *Washington Post* described his step back in time to join a Salafi group:

> When I was 16, I found myself assailed by doubts about the existence of God. I prayed to God to give me the strength to overcome them. I made a deal with Him: I would give up everything, devote myself to Him and live the way the prophet Muhammad and his companions had lived 1,400 years ago if He would rid me of my doubts.
>
> I joined a hard-line Salafi group. I abandoned modern life and lived in a mud hut, apart from my family. Viewing modern education as corrupt and immoral, I joined a circle of scholars who taught the Islamic sciences in the classical way, just as

they had been taught 1,200 years ago. My involvement with this group led me to violence, and landed me in prison. In 1991, I took part in fire-bombing video stores in Riyadh and a women's center in my home town of Buraidah. . . .

By the time I turned 26 . . . my eyes were opened to the hypocrisy of so many who held themselves out as Muslim role models. I saw Islamic judges ignoring the marks of torture borne by my prison comrades. I learned of Islamic teachers who molested their students. I heard devout Muslims who never missed the five daily prayers lying with ease to people who did not share their extremist beliefs . . . . Muslims have the right to question and criticize our religious leaders and not to take everything they tell us for granted.[29]

Saudi Arabian madrassas consistently and devotedly

teach Wahhabism beliefs. A *New York Times* article by journalist Neil MacFarquhar stated:

> The textbook for one of the five religion classes required of all 10th graders in Saudi public high schools tackles the complicated issue of who good Muslims should befriend.
>
> After examining a number of scriptures which warn of the dangers of having Christian and Jewish friends, the lesson concludes: "It is compulsory for the Muslims to be loyal to each other and to consider the infidels their enemy."
>
> . . . "If you review the curriculum in Saudi Arabia, you would see that it promotes any kind of extremist views of Islam, even in the eyes of very devout Muslims," said Abdul Khadir Tash, the editor of Al Bilad newspaper.[30]

Imams and ayatollahs have referred to Jews as monkeys and pigs and have called for them to be "wiped off the face of the earth." Others have sympathized with the 9/11 terrorists and celebrated openly as the towers crashed to the ground in New York City. While this may not correspond to the beliefs of the royalty in the Saudi Kingdom, few are willing to challenge the Wahhabists and Salafists. Criticizing either is considered a direct affront to both.

Reporters on the PBS television show "Frontline" interviewed several individuals regarding the impact of madrassas, or religious schools, on Islam. They revealed the following:

> Many of the Taliban were educated in Saudi-financed madrassas in Pakistan that teach Wahhabism, a particularly austere and rigid form of Islam which is rooted in Saudi Arabia. Around the world, Saudi wealth and charities contributed to an explosive growth of madrassas during the Afghan jihad against the Soviets. During that war (1979-1989), a new kind of madrassa emerged in the Pakistan-Afghanistan region—not so much concerned about scholarship as

making war on infidels. The enemy
then was the Soviet Union, today it's
America.[31]

Vali Nasr, an expert on Islamic fundamentalist
reported:

> In order to have terrorists, in
> order to have supporters for terror-
> ists, in order to have people who are
> willing to interpret religion in violent
> ways, in order to have people who are
> willing to legitimate crashing your-
> self into a building and killing 5,000
> innocent people, you need particular
> interpretations of Islam.
>
> Those interpretations of Islam are
> being propagated out of schools that
> receive organizational and financial
> funding from Saudi Arabia. In fact,
> I would push it further: that these
> schools would not have existed with-
> out Saudi funding. They would not
> have proliferated across Pakistan
> and India and Afghanistan without

Saudi funding. They would not have had the kind of prowess that they have without Saudi funding, and they would not have trained as many people without Saudi funding.[32]

When questioned about who attends the Saudi-supported fundamentalist madrassas, the answer was:

They are recruited from among the lower classes and lower-middle classes . . . . There are peasant children from the peasant backgrounds . . . . That's why the ideology that's propagated by these schools is so significant in shaping minds in the Muslim world. So if regular schooling is not schooling people, and schools that propagate fanaticism are schooling people, it doesn't take a brain surgeon to figure out what would be the impact on society.[33]

Salafism, like Wahhabism, can be found at the core of the Islamic State formed by a 2004 break from al Qaeda in Iraq. It spread from that war-torn country into Syria, another nation overrun by revolution. It was the perfect petri dish for terrorism to morph into an even more violent mutation. It has now spread its tentacles into Lebanon, Egypt, France, Germany and the United States.

As stated in one report:

> With few exceptions, German jihadists are males under the age of 25 who have been radicalized by Salafist propaganda, according to Michael Kiefer, a German Islam expert who teaches at the government-sponsored Institute for Islamic Theology at the University of Osnabrück.[54]

Despite weak protests against terrorism, the Saudis have for the past fifty years supported Sunni Salafism in the form of IS in Syria and Iraq, al Qaeda in many countries, Boko Haram in Nigeria, and al-Shabab in Somalia—some of the most vicious and aggressive terrorist organizations worldwide.

4

IDEOLOGICAL
WARFARE

We're not in the middle of a war on terror . . . .
We're not facing an axis of evil. Instead, we are in
the midst of an ideological conflict. We are facing
. . . . loose confederation of people who believe in a
perverted stream of Islam . . . . Terrorism is just the
means they use to win converts to their cause.[35]

DAVID BROOKS,
JOURNALIST

THE CLASH OF IDEOLOGIES between the Western world
and Islam is a highly visible collision. The West is rooted
in the concepts of the Bible and belief in the deity of Jesus
Christ. The Scriptures teach that those who govern do so by
the hand of God to maintain order. Romans 13:1-3, NKJV,
gives us this direction:

Let every soul be subject to the governing authorities. For there is no authority except from God, and the authorities that exist are appointed by God. Therefore whoever resists the authority resists the ordinance of God, and those who resist will bring judgment on themselves. For rulers are not a terror to good works, but to evil. Do you want to be unafraid of the authority? Do what is good, and you will have praise from the same.

Radical Islamists employ brutal acts using suicide bombings and other gruesome forms of violence—beheadings, immolation, crucifixion—to reach their objectives.

British author and philosopher Roger Scruton wrote:

The Muslim conception of holy law, pointing the unique way to salvation, and applying to every area of human life, involves a *confiscation of the political.* Those matters which, in Western societies, are resolved by negotiation, compromise, and the

laborious work of offices and com-
mittees are [under Islamic rule] the
object of immovable and eternal
decrees, either laid down explicitly
in [the Koran], or discerned there by
some religious figurehead. (Emphasis in original)[36]

Ideological warfare did not find its beginnings with
IS; the roots of ideological warfare were deeply imbedded
in the mind and proffered in the writings of Adolf Hitler
in the years leading up to World War II. During his early
time in Vienna, he immersed himself in publications that
preached anti-Semitism.[37] Following the end of World
War I, Hitler joined the *Nationalsozialistische Deutsche
Arbeiterpartei*, or Nazi Party. He eventually assumed
leadership of the organization and transformed it into the
"instrument of [his own] policies."[38] Hitler would later
write his missive, *Mein Kampf*, the book in which he out-
lined his hate-filled, anti-Semitic rhetoric aimed at the
Jewish people.

It was this pompous posturing that drove the little
dictator's policies. Author Richard Evans wrote, "Hitler
considered racial conflict . . . the essence of history, and

the Jews to be the sworn enemy of the German race."[39]
Hitler informed František Chvalkovský, foreign minister
of Czechoslovakia, "We are going to destroy the Jews."[40]
And he and his henchmen made a brazen attempt that
nearly succeeded.

Mein Kampf is even today a widely-read and quoted
tome in some Arabic circles[41], therefore, is it any wonder
that Hitler's brand of ideological warfare is practiced by
the leaders of various terror organizations? Just as its
message was key to driving Hitler's dedicated followers,
so it is still fundamental to many who desire the annihilation of Jews—not just those who escaped the clutches of
the Nazis, but Jews worldwide.

When people today talk of Islamic ideological warfare,
it most often refers to the doctrines of fanatical Salafists
waging jihad. The sect rose from being virtually unknown
to having become a worldwide offshoot of Islam. One of
the basic tenets of Salafism is that Shia Muslims are plot-
ting with the "Great Satan"—the United States—to restrict
Sunnis in the Middle East. It is here that the two civilizations collide, and the differences between the two are
most evident.

The shared Western beliefs of democracy, the rule
of law, religious tolerance, and freedom of speech are

considered by most to be superior to the fascism, violence, and the glamorization of wanton death utilized by groups like the Islamic State. Western leaders and the public in general need to realize the power, importance, and superiority of our ideological weapons. Life, liberty, and the pursuit of happiness will always be preferable to the death, despotism, and misery of our radical Islamic adversaries.

Russ Read, a member of a Washington, D.C. think tank believes:

> While the battlefield of ideology seems uncertain, there is a silver lining. In addition to our kinetic weapons being superior to our adversary, so too are our ideological ones.
>
> The Western world, and the U.S. in particular, needs to realize that it is ok to be proud of our ideals, and in turn protect them. For far too long we have allowed our good graces to get the better of us; we have essentially become apologetic in practicing and defending our beliefs.
>
> Instead of uniting together against

a common enemy, Western leaders try and put our adversaries on a morally equivalent plane and explain away their actions. *Just because we in the West believe in everyone's right to their opinion, it does not mean that everyone's opinion is right.* (Emphasis mine)[42]

Response from Western allies following a terror attack has been half-hearted to say the least. One country may rise up in indignation and retaliate, but the anger is soon pacified and replaced with attempts at conciliation. Such appeasement is the offshoot of self-loathing; we hate war. General William Tecumseh Sherman said, "War is hell." Rather than believe those who wage war against us are evil, we sometimes mistakenly begin to see *ourselves* as evil for retaliating, or even worse, preemptively striking to prevent a sure danger to regional or world security. Self-loathing replaces righteous indignation—and begets pacification.

The desire of our leaders to negotiate no matter the cost gives rise to those in the West who become unwitting cohorts to the jihadists. These individuals rationalize the presence of evil and attacks by terrorists based on their perception of punishment for America's past sins.

The result is unconcern, self-righteousness, or lack of motivation—the disorder has many names. Whatever the label, it results in simply not taking the threat of terror attacks seriously. The first World Trade Center attack in 1993 should have been a wake-up call; instead, few realized the import of that momentous explosion: It was a precursor to 9/11.

If we refuse to act now—before terrorists gain further access to nuclear weapons—for what will the 9/11 attacks be a precursor? If we cast aside the principles that have made this nation great, we have no hope of winning the ideological war, for we will have demolished the building blocks of a democratic society.

There is only one way to win in this clash of civilizations. Winston Churchill understood this when he spoke these unforgettable words before Parliament on June 4, 1940, following the dark days of defeat at Dunkirk in which 338,000 Allied troops had to be evacuated to English shores:

> Even though large tracts of Europe
> and many old and famous States have

fallen or may fall into the grip of the Gestapo and all the odious apparatus of Nazi rule, we shall not flag or fail. We shall go on to the end, we shall fight in France, we shall fight on the seas and oceans, we shall fight with growing confidence and growing strength in the air, we shall defend our Island, whatever the cost may be, we shall fight on the beaches, we shall fight on the landing grounds, we shall fight in the fields and in the streets, we shall fight in the hills; we shall never surrender.[43]

The terror of 9/11 immediately captured our collective awareness, but only briefly. Our attention span seems to be measured in nanoseconds rather than the years it will take to achieve victory in this struggle. We tend to ridicule the ragtag armies of many of the world's superpower pretenders—Iran being a case in point.

In a television interview with Chuck Todd on NBC's "Meet the Press," President Obama was asked to address the subject of the Islamic State. The president's reply was:

The analogy we use around here sometimes, and I think is accurate, is if a jayvee [junior varsity] team puts on Lakers uniforms that doesn't make them Kobe Bryant . . . . think there is a distinction between the capacity and reach of a bin Laden and a network that is actively planning major terrorist plots against the homeland versus jihadists who are engaged in various local power struggles and disputes, often sectarian.[44]

Mr. Obama later claimed he was not specifically referring to the Islamic State.

We refuse to admit that the U.S., like Israel, could suddenly become a repository for suicide-belted jihads intent on our destruction. We dismiss as mere nuisances the threats made by the likes of Iran's Ayatollah Ali Khamenei. After all, what weapons might the fanatical practitioners of Islam really have at their disposal? Namely:

- ✧ Weapons of mass destruction, or the ability to obtain them;

- ✧ Rabid religious fanaticism;

- ✧ Funds flowing into their coffers from oil-rich Middle Eastern countries such as Saudi Arabia and Iran, among others;

- ✧ Broad appeal—from beggars in the streets to university professors in the halls of academia; from Baghdad to Boston; from Tehran to Toronto;

- ✧ Immigration and infiltration—legal immigrants to largely non-Muslim countries such as the United States, Great Britain, France, Germany, Canada, and Spain are well versed in using the legal and political systems in those countries to further their agenda of ultimate domination;

- ✧ Sheer numbers—if the radical element of Islam measures only ten percent of Muslims as a whole, that number is still a staggering 125 million plus Islamic Infidels. That is a sizeable army of radicals with only one ultimate aim: to kill infidels wherever they may be found.

Will the lack of resolve, the self-loathing, and the absence of motivation cause the U.S. to abandon the war on terror? Will the West ultimately fall victim to disastrous losses of human life and goods? How long will it take to recognize the truth that no one, I repeat, *no one*— no American, Britain, Frenchman, German, Spaniard, not even many Muslims—is safe from the assault of the radical Islamists' hatred? And the most pressing question of all: Can the civilized world survive the onslaught of such fanaticism? What will it take to jar the West out of its comfortable complacency? I pray it is not another devastating attack or series of attacks on U.S. soil.

The West has become a league of nations whose focus is instant gratification—"We want it now!" Idealistically, an attack against the enemy should be launched after breakfast with astounding results by nightly news time. Much of the interim is spent arguing about tactics and political ramifications. What seems to be lost in translation is that there is a growing bloc of people out there who want only one thing: world domination by radical Islamists who 1) are not reasonable; and 2) have no interest in compromise.

How can the men and women who are charged with protecting the citizens of their countries persuade themselves that their "one and done" forays into IS territory will stop the carnage? As noted earlier, the first, unsuccessful attack on the World Trade Center was in 1993.

Bin Laden and his cronies plotted and postponed another attack for *eight years* before successfully bringing down, not only the two World Trade Center towers, but leaving a devastating smoking chasm in the Pentagon.

In order to win the ideological war against Salafism and Wahhabism, the West must make a commitment to set a course and stay it. It will be long, hard and costly, but the alternative is a Western world under the thumb of sharia law where the word "liberty" has no real meaning, and "democracy" is only a dim vision of the past.

5

TERROR AND SOCIAL MEDIA

It has been said that journalists are terrorists' best friends, because they are willing to give terrorist operations maximum exposure. This is not to say that journalists as a group are sympathetic to terrorists, although it may appear so. It simply means that violence is news, whereas peace and harmony are not. The terrorists need the media, and the media find in terrorism all the ingredients of an exciting story.[45]

JOHN WHITEHEAD,
CONSTITUTIONAL ATTORNEY

ON MONDAY, APRIL 15, 2013, two obscure Islamic jihadist brothers became superstars thanks to the U.S. media. When pictures of Tamerlan Tsarnaev and his younger brother, Dzhokhar, were released during the manhunt in Boston, some were outraged at the photo of Dzhokhar "taken when he was about 14. Soft, angelic, nice little boy. Harmless. Cute. Big, loveable eyes."[46] It certainly did not depict the young man who callously positioned his back-pack of explosives to snuff out the life of a child standing nearby and maiming and injuring countless others. It was outrageous! Terrorism is the only business worldwide that enjoys free advertising; every other client must pay for it.

To spread terror, one has to spread the *news* of terror. The only mechanism capable of doing so significantly is the media. Why would news sources in the U.S. fuel and feed terror, and immortalize terrorists? "If it bleeds, it leads," is the motto of big business media worldwide.

The United States differs vastly from Israel in that Israel does not do that! When an act of terrorism is committed, neither the name nor face of the terrorist appears in newspapers or on television—just the opposite is true. Everything possible is done to marginalize and make the perpetrator irrelevant. Yes, the act is reported, but it does not name or reward the terrorist.

Rather than glorify the jihadists, Israel glorifies the victims and constructs the story around them. In spite of the fact that it is a very difficult name to spell or pronounce, everyone knows it was the Tsarnaev brothers who committed that cowardly act in Boston. The vast majority of Americans do not know the name Martin William Richard. He was the little eight year-old boy who died from the blast of the bomb that was placed just a few feet from him. His beloved mother, Denise, sustained brain injuries, and his six year-old sister, Jane, lost a leg.

It is vitally important that would-be terrorists come to believe their demented, demonic acts will usher them into disgrace, not a media paradise. The U.S. media needs to be held accountable. Companies that sponsor news programs need to come under pressure from the American public with demands that media aggrandizement of terror be stopped. It is not the victim that must change in order for terror to end.

The obsession of wanting to understand "why" Islamic Infidels desire to kill us is part of the problem. The secular humanistic media, by obsessing over the why, elevates the jihadist while it castigates the victim. It makes it seem as if the victims caused the problem while the perpetrators are depicted as both innocent and exploited. The belief seems to be that bad acts must be blamed on societal, psychological or economic circumstances. Or worse, the unspoken mantra: We have met the enemy and he is us.

Seldom will you hear the secular media using the

"T" word, terrorist, or the "J" word, jihadist, or the "I" word, Islamic—and certainly not the appellation, "Islamic Infidel." The media seems, rather, obsessed with tolerance and political correctness. Terrorists kill the body, but the secular, New Age media kills the soul.

I, for one, would be delighted if the U.S. were to adopt a policy that excluded any personal information about every terrorist who threatens our country, but this will never happen. At the very least, we need to end the symbiotic relationship between terrorists and the media. Why? The success of an attack is measured by the number of those who sit before electronic devices—television, iPad, iPhone, or computer—and view the devastating aftermath. The more coverage, the more free advertising for the jihadists, the bigger the draw that sparks the desire to join the ranks of the terrorists.

Social media outlets have also become a draw for jihadist communicators—Google, Twitter, Instagram, Facebook and others. Islamic Infidels worldwide have become adept at employing the Internet as a tool against its inventors—those in the West. According to an article from the Council on Foreign Relations, social media sites are a powerful means for recruitment:

The Internet is a powerful tool for terrorists, who use online message boards and chat rooms to share information, coordinate attacks, spread propaganda, raise funds, and recruit, experts say. According to Haifa University's Gabriel Weimann, whose research on the subject is widely cited, the number of terrorist sites increased exponentially over the last decade—from less than 100 to more than 4,800 two years ago. The numbers can be somewhat misleading, however. In the case of al-Qaeda, hundreds of sister sites have been promulgated but only a handful are considered active, experts say. Nonetheless, analysts do see a clear proliferation trend.

Terrorist websites can serve as virtual training grounds, offering tutorials on building bombs, firing surface-to-air missiles, shooting at

U.S. soldiers, and sneaking into Iraq from abroad . . . .

Perhaps the most effective way in which terrorists use the Internet is the spread of propaganda. Abu Musab al-Zarqawi's al-Qaeda cell in Iraq has proven particularly adept in its use of the web, garnering attention by posting footage of roadside bombings, the decapitation of American hostage Nick Berg, and kidnapped Egyptian and Algerian diplomats prior to their execution . . . . The Internet also provides a global pool of potential recruits and donors. Online terrorist fundraising has become so commonplace that some organizations are able to accept donations via the popular online payment service PayPal.[47]

The Anti-Defamation League (ADL) relates that Islamic Infidels often utilize social media to distribute anti-American and anti-Israel misinformation. According to the ADL report:

Several Internet sites created by Hamas supporters, for example, carry the organization's charter and its political and military communiqués, some of which openly call for and extol the murder of Jews . . . . Still others use the Internet to raise funds; Hezbollah, for example, the pro-Iranian Shiite terrorist organization based in south Lebanon, sells books and publications through its Web site.

Some Israeli and U.S. officials believe that terrorists from Hamas and Islamic Jihad use the Internet to provide specific instructions to fellow terrorists including maps, photographs, directions, codes and technical details of how to use explosives.[48]

Mount Holyoke College once released a paper entitled, "Why Terrorists Use the Internet." The document listed several dynamics of why social media is the weapon of choice:

The determining factor in whether terrorists turn to the internet or not is whether it promotes their goals. There are five goals of a terrorist organization, as defined by Ernest Evans, a research associate at the Brookings Institute. They are:

1. To publicize its cause on a regional and international level.

2. To harass and intimidate authorities to force them to make concessions.

3. To polarize society in order to bring down the regime.

4. To aggravate relations between states or nations.

5. To free political prisoners and secure monetary ransoms to finance their cause.[49]

In October 2014, three teenaged girls from Denver, Colorado stole $2,000 from their parents and boarded a plane for Germany. There, they planned to transfer to a flight for Turkey where they were determined to join ISIS. The girls had apparently been seduced by Internet videos and social media messages. A CNN story identified the search for a "sense of belonging" as the reason many young men and women try to reach Syria:

> "It's more than just a radical interpretation of Islam that is drawing teens to the extremely bloodthirsty militant group," a former CIA officer says.
>
> "They're often times searching for an identity, because what the jihadis are actually pushing is a specific narrative, which is: Your people (Muslims) are being oppressed in this place called Syria; your government is doing nothing; we're the only ones who are actually going to help you out," said Aki Peritz. "Why don't you join the fight?"
>
> Richard Barrett of The Soufan Group says many of the teens lack a sense of belonging where they live, and they believe ISIS can give it to them.

"The general picture provided by foreign fighters of their lives in Syria suggests camaraderie, good morale and purposeful activity, all mixed in with a sense of understated heroism, designed to attract their friends as well as to boost their own self-esteem," he says.[50]

This indoctrination, this enticement to excitement is all made possible by the media—social, print, and broadcast. These outlets have made it easier to showcase the very Islamic Infidels who would quash those outlets if successful in their determination to found a caliphate based on sharia law. The media would be silenced; social networks restricted; and freedom would be dead and buried.

The emergence of a web of networked Islamic Infidel jihadists who propagate their doctrine, distribute their stories and engender loyalty has made the spread of terrorism more proficient and opportune and even more difficult to track, arrest and prosecute. It is time to stop the media exploitation of terrorism and stop giving these terrorists a name and a platform.

6

WHY DO THEY
HATE US?

The root cause of terrorism lies not in grievances,
but in a disposition toward unbridled violence. This
can be traced to a world view which asserts that
certain ideological and religious goals justify, indeed
demand, the shedding of all moral inhibitions.

PRIME MINISTER BENJAMIN NETANYAHU[51]

QUESTIONS WE OFTEN HEAR in response to terror attacks by Islamic Infidels are: Why do they hate us? Why do they want to kill us? The answer is both simple and complex, and a matter on which a plethora of psychologists could expend hours of energy in search of a resolution. The simple answer is: The United States, and by association, other Western countries plus Israel are obstructions on their superhighway to the establishment of an Islamic caliphate—and total domination.

If, as some have ascertained, many Muslims are peace-loving and have no argument with us, what propels jihad-ists over the edge into extreme loathing and brutality? Is it, as some have intimated, poverty and ignorance? Not neccessarily! Mohammed Emwazi, the individual known by the appellation of "Jihadi John," is thought to have been responsible for the beheading of American, British, Syrian and Japanese hostages of the Islamic State. Emwazi was the well-educated son of a middle-class family that had relocated from Kuwait to London—no ignorance or pov-erty there. Why did his search for answers in his own life lead him to join the ranks of other Islamic Infidels? He took the answer to that question to his grave.

Unlike others who have examined this question, I don't believe the total resolution is tied to searching for the meaning of life, or American politics abroad, or even U.S. support for Israel. Nor is it likely because of our air bases in Western Europe or Turkey.

They hate us because we have freedom—of religion, education and speech. We practice tolerance toward others—except perhaps those who are determined to hoist our heads on stakes. We decry those who kill for the sake of killing; who enslave for the sake of humiliating another. We are hated because we have shunned the teachings of Islam and embraced Christianity.

Journalist and producer Bridget Gabriel, wrote in her book, *Because they Hate*:

> They hate our way of life. They hate our freedom. They hate our democracy. They hate the practice of every religion but their own. They don't just disagree. They *hate*. Not just Judaism. Not just Christianity. In various parts of the world today, Islamists are also waging terror war against Hindus, Buddhists, and all other "infidels." The imposition of Islam upon the entire world is not merely their goal. It is their religious duty.[52]

In 1964, Ronald Reagan delivered a speech titled, "A Time for Choosing." He said of our great nation:

> You and I have the courage to say to our enemies, "There is a price we will not pay." There is a point beyond

which they must not advance . . . . You
and I have a rendezvous with des-
tiny. We will preserve for our children this, the last best hope of man
on Earth, or we will sentence them
to take the last step into a thousand
years of darkness.[53]

Many Muslims are not opposed to democracy—as
noted by statistics that the majority of Muslims are not
Islamic Infidels. They simply want to live freely by the dic-
tates of their own conscience just as the rest of the world
does. Jihadists do not, and will do anything to keep Islam
under radical control and moving toward a caliphate gov-
erned by sharia law.

But the question remains: "Is America strong enough
to achieve victory over Islamic Infidels?" I am concerned
that it is not. The U.S. certainly has the technology, but
does it have the will to stay the course until victory is
realized? Can the American people overcome the seeming
lack of will to win, the self-loathing, and the unconcern
that seems to surround the War on Terror?

There have been times in our history when failure
to stand our ground would have rendered unthinkable

consequences. This is a time when ignorance is not bliss—it is deadly. The threat is very real; negotiating with a group of Islamic Infidels who have no fear of death but see only imagined rewards is the very definition of insanity.

The Liberal Left has convinced many Americans that the War on Terror cannot be won through military action and has shattered our will to win. On June 18, 1940, when faced with the real danger that Hitler's troops could invade Britain during World War II, Winston Churchill addressed the people of his country. He concluded with a warning of what would happen if the British people failed to rebuff the German dictator:

> But if we fail, then the whole world, including the United States, including all that we have known and cared for, will sink into the abyss of a new Dark Age made more sinister, and perhaps more protracted, by the lights of perverted science.[54]

It is a warning that should still reverberate today, and especially with the determination of Islamic Infidels to kill and destroy.

The Western world must NOT lose its resolve with

the thought that these jihadists will simply pick up their marbles, give up the fight for a worldwide caliphate and go home. Sense and sensibility needs to step to the forefront. A united stand against this threat is required lest all of humanity be dragged backward into the Dark Ages of hopelessness.

There is one point that must not be overlooked, and that is the religious aspects of why they hate us. Bruce Walker, a writer for *The American Thinker*, revealed the cause:

> There is another divide, however, and that is based upon fidelity to the traditions of Judeo-Christianity and contempt for that moral system. Recall that the same Obama group which quickly blamed riots and murder [in Bengazi] upon an anti-Islamic film recently created a Democratic Party platform in which God and Jerusalem had been wholly omitted, and then had convention members jeer when those two vital words were put into the platform.

Religious Americans are much more likely to support Romney and oppose Obama.

There is a vast divide of faith which separates conservative Americans and Israelis on one side and the rest of mankind, which hates them, on the other. Americans are profoundly religious, and despite a full court press by secular progressives over sixty years, "Red State" America is much more religious than "Blue State" America—and America, taken as a whole, is dramatically more religious than European nations, with the percentage of Americans who consider religion "very important" 50%, compared to 22% in Spain, 21% in Germany, 17% in Britain, and 13% in France.[55]

How can we more effectively neutralize the hatred that is vomited up by Islamic Infidels in the Middle East? The United States—leaders, diplomats, and citizens alike—should realize that there is an ongoing contest between the ideology of democracy and that of Islamic law. Burying our collective heads in the sand only means that we are resistant to the truth. We need to send a strong and vibrant message to every Arab nation that the United States is comprised of people who are kind and compassionate, who abhor random hostilities, who genuinely believe in the value of learning and the implementation of economic possibilities.

Bridget Gabriel reminds us of the danger of Liberal Left apathy:

Our leaders and politicians bend over backward to tell us how sweetly wonderful Islam is and that most Muslims are moderate, that a few radicals have hijacked this unbelievably sweet poetry called the Koran and are trying to twist it to do harm. Snap out of it, America. America and the West can no longer afford to stay in a state of ignorance. The consequences of this mental laziness are starting to attack the body of our

country, and if the necessary medi-
cal steps aren't taken now to control
it, death will be knocking soon . . . .
Muslims are telling us exactly what
they plan . . . straight out what their
goal is to conquer us and establish
Islamic law in Western lands. They
are following through on every word
they have said so far.[56]

The truth is that before 9/11, most Americans were
kind and openhearted and believed in the inherent good
of our fellowman. The plane that plowed into the North
Tower of the World Trade Center changed that outlook
forever. That has only been reinforced by the fanatical
Islamic Infidels who continue to deliver death, destruction, and devastation. If you were to challenge the young
members of IS regarding why they wanted to kill anyone
who disagreed with them, I suspect the answer would be
"power and control." It would have little to do with past
tangible or imagined offenses.

7

ISIS: A GRAVE DANGER TO ISRAEL

The Israeli Arab Conflict is not about geography but about Jew hatred. Throughout the Islamic as well as Christendom's history Jews have been persecuted; the persecution of Israel is just the same as the old anti-Semitism . . . The Arab refugees are being used as pawns to create a terror breeding ground, as a form of aggression against Israel.[57]

WALID SHOEBAT,
FORMER PLO MEMBER

THE ONLY NATION that restrains the conflagration of Islamic terrorism in the West is Israel. She is the firewall between America and the anti-Semitic Islamic nations. I strongly believe that America's ability to win the war on terrorism is directly related to our willingness to support Israel's fight against terrorism.

A less often asked question that might be considered is: If Israel were no longer a major player in the Middle East, who would the Arab countries blame for the Palestinian unrest, for the unrepressed hatred between the Sunni and Shia factions, and for the terrorist attacks which encircle the globe? Or, if the Palestinian issue were to disappear tomorrow, were all the Palestinian refugees absorbed by other Arab countries, would Israel be recognized by the Arab League as a legitimate Middle East state? Or would another pretext be found to continue the onslaught against the Jewish people and their homeland?

If that were to happen, would the antipathy toward America, the "Great Satan" come to a halt? Islamic Infidel terrorists consider America to be a Christian nation, and as such, fair game. Would Israel, the "Little Satan," still be considered a usurper and a target for terrorism?

The United States has endeavored to utilize Israel, the tiny democratic state in the midst of a sea of instability in the Middle East, as a bulwark in deterring communism, fascism, and terrorism. The U.S. liaison with Arab countries is one of convenience and economics: The mortal enemy of Israel brought countless barrels of black gold (oil) to the table and uses it still today to intimidate the United States.

As Middle Eastern oil flows to the West, arms are shipped back in the other direction. In fact, the Middle East region is currently the United States' number one client for weapons of war. Even after the deadly events of September 11, 2001 petrodollars earned by countries such as Saudi Arabia, Iran, and Libya have been utilized to sponsor terrorism, produce weapons of mass destruction, and finance a gospel of hatred that is employed to brainwash millions of Islamic youth. America's leaders have been unwilling to admit that we are being blackmailed, let alone drawing a firm line in the sand against extortion. It's time to stand up to these bullies and stop capitulating to coercion; the future of our nation depends on it.

Knowing Islamic fundamentalists are hell-bent on annihilating the tiny country, Israel has developed the fourth largest nuclear arsenal in the world. Israeli leaders are determined that what happened during the Holocaust will never happen again. It has long been known that Israel has had nuclear strike capabilities since at least the late 1960s. Today, in addition to Pakistan, another Islamic nation, Iran, is very close to having a finger poised over the red button as well.

Through these two political—and spiritual—liaisons, the U.S. has stepped into the center of a prophetic storm.

She now finds herself trying to accommodate Jew-haters who have refused even to acknowledge the very existence of the State of Israel. The U.S. has chosen to appease with both bombs and *baksheesh* (bribes) as more than $400 billion in military equipment and over $100 billion in aid has been dispatched to various Arab countries.

Our modern secular world is still conflicted by the relationship between science and religion—which most assume was won by secular science. Suddenly, a religious adversary is attacking secular America. It's no longer just the streets of Jerusalem that are threatened, but those of New York, Washington, Boston, and who knows how many other cities.

In my book, *Beyond Iraq: The Next Move*, I stated my belief that weapons of mass destruction were in Syria. It took U.S. officials almost a year to be willing to admit that.

The Middle East Review of International Affairs (MERIA) released pictures in July 2014 of Kurds appearing to have been gassed by ISIL troops. According to journalist Paul Alster:

> That fighting came just one
> month after Islamic State forces
> surged through the once-notorious

Muthanna compound in Iraq, the massive base where Hussein began producing chemical weapons in the 1980s, which he used to kill thousands of Kurds in Halabja in northern Iraq in 1988. Experts believe the chemical weapons were used on July 12, in the village of Avidko, close to Kobani, the Kurdish town on the Turkish border that is now the scene of fierce fighting between Kurds and Islamic State forces. If Islamic State fighters did indeed gain chemical weapons in Muthanna, it would corroborate a 2007 CIA report that confirmed their presence there. That report was cited when, in June, Islamic State fighters captured the Muthanna facility from Iraqi soldiers and allegedly seized a cache of chemical weapons, including more than 2,500 degraded chemical rockets contaminated with deadly mustard gas. If Islamic State has chemical weapons, they also could have obtained them in Syria, where embattled President Bashar Assad has as many as 16 factories for making deadly chemical weapons, despite pledging to get rid of them under pressure from the West.[58]

Former *New York Post* columnist Arthur Ahlert added:

The latest revelations on the details of Saddam's weapons stockpile, now potentially in the hands of Sunni radicals, affirm the Bush administration's characterization of Iraq as a territory situated in a hotbed of radicalism, flooded with a bevy of highly dangerous weapons and overseen by a criminal rogue regime. Indeed, the WMDs are to say nothing of the Hussein government's nuclear weapons program, also put to a stop by intervention in Iraq . . . . the latest details of Saddam's WMD stockpile—something there can be no doubt that the Secretary of State [John Kerry, former member of the Senate Committee on Foreign Relations] was aware of—exposes yet again the left's great deception on the danger of Hussein and the motivation behind the Iraq war.[59]

With IS on the march, it is a direct challenge to the Shia populations of Syria, Iraq, and Iran. Would there not be a certain amount of irony if, years after Saddam Hussein's regime had been declared WMD-free, chemical and biological weapons were finally found in Syria in the hands of those terrorist groups? Iraqi general Georges Sada, second in command of the Iraq Air Force who served under Hussein, has stated unequivocally that Saddam's undiscovered cache of WMDs had been transported into Syria for safekeeping. Who can fathom the horror of such weapons falling into the hands of Islamic Infidels?

This is one of many reasons Israel must be allowed to fight the war against terrorism that it has never been free to pursue. Sadly, it will undoubtedly be forced to do so alone. Israel is surrounded by enemies and must be allowed to root out the terrorist organizations that threaten her. The war on terrorism will never be won as long as Syria, Lebanon, Gaza, and the Palestinian territories remain points of exportation for suicide bombers.

True hope for peace lies in discerning the truth and acting on it, not in believing myths propagated by liberal power brokers that incite Jew-hatred. Too many people in the U.S. view the real enemy as "narrow-minded, right-wing, Bible-thumping Christians" who believe in black and white, right and wrong. The same people who see conservative Christians as the enemy often legitimize the acts of cold-blooded murderers as a means to obtain freedom and peace. These apostles of appeasement have raised the hopes of the Islamic Infidels so high that the national security of the United States is now at stake, and equally important, our very freedoms at risk.

Many believe the current Palestinian crisis has much to do with the issue of Jew-hatred, and so it does. The entire Palestinian crisis can be attributed to two things— refugees and terrorism.

Is there another refugee crisis anywhere on earth that has drawn the world into such a mess? The answer clearly is, "No." How did Israel solve its refugee crisis in Europe at the end of the Holocaust? How did it resolve the crisis in Arab countries where Jewish citizens were being killed? It simply took care of its own.

Civilized countries solve refugee crises on their own; conversely, the Arab world has fueled and fed the Palestinian refugee crisis to exploit Jew-hatred. Their attitude is: "Blame the Jews for all problems, just as Hitler did, and we will not be held accountable for our brutality." Since these "thugocracies" are run by the bullet, and not the ballot, someone needs to bear the blame. Why not the Jews in Israel and the so-called crusaders in the United States?

The U.S. has done little, if anything, to address this danger that must be stopped. Every possible means available must be employed to shut down the Islamic Infidels who kill in the name of Allah. Some have even recruited children and used them as suicide bombers, mine sweepers, and decoys.

Many worldwide believe that the terror crisis is a result of the Palestinian issue. If the terror crisis were a result of that dispute, it could be resolved by the Arab League, the nations which turned their collective backs on the very refugees it created. Why did it initiate the myth that Israeli Arabs must have a separate state inside Israel, even though a Palestinian state has never existed?

These refugees were told that Egyptian-born billionaire terrorist Yasser Arafat was their "George Washington." Why? The answer: the U.S. then began to tolerate subtle anti-Semitism perpetrated in the name of establishing a Palestinian state. It is a bigotry presently polluting and poisoning the peace of the world. The war on terrorism cannot be won without a war against such prejudice.

The United States struggles to remain the mightiest nation on earth and has long been a partaker of God's blessings. During the past few decades, America has allowed her culture to become polluted, attempted to dethrone God, and defiled her heroes. Bible-believing Americans have been demonized as bigots and extremists. The name of God has been removed from schools, courts, and town squares, and some have even tried to erase His name from our coins—"in God we trust"—from the Pledge of Allegiance—"one nation, under God." The same moral compromise infecting our domestic policy has also tainted our foreign policy: the U.S. annually sends foreign aid to such terrorist-harboring countries as Egypt, Iraq, Jordan, Pakistan, West Bank/Gaza, Indonesia, and Somalia.

If Americans do not wake up to the truth, the U.S. political machine will continue on a collision course with prophecy. Many believe there is nothing we can do about it; that if it is foretold, it must come to pass. However, we could be missing the true point of prophecy. The Bible doesn't tell us what the future holds so that we can sit back and allow disaster to strike; but rather so that we can take any necessary actions to make sure we are on the prophetic side of blessing. In the Old Testament God often warned His people of impending disaster—not just so they would know it was coming, but to give them an opportunity for repentance and restoration. It is up to God-fearing Americans willing to step out and make a difference to keep our country headed in the right direction in both domestic and foreign policy. Do we truly think we can move our government forward without His guidance? Our forefathers certainly did not!

Sooner or later everyone on this planet—rich and poor, skeptic and religious, president and pauper—will be forced to think about eternity. Can we really plan for the future—of our nation, our world—without considering it? While democracy may have been conceived in Greece, it was not until Bible-believing, God-fearing people joined together to form the United States of America that it has risen to the ideal it has become today. Our governmental structure may not be perfect, but it is the best our world has seen, and all because it was founded as a system defined by moral clarity, and based upon biblical principles.

Dr. Martin Luther King Jr. said, "Nothing in the world is more dangerous than sincere ignorance and conscientious stupidity."[60] The U.S. entered the twenty-first century with a terminal case of both. Our nation is in this position primarily because of its alliances. The descendants of Abraham—Isaac and Ishmael—are still in a struggle for dominion, and the U.S. has stumbled right into the middle of it.

Ancient scriptures have a great deal to say about the two spirits behind this battle. Ishmael was not the son of promise, but the son of a man ignoring God's will and going his own way. God had promised Abraham a son, but his wife Sarah was barren. At her insistence, Abraham took Hagar, her maidservant, and impregnated her. Ishmael was the result of that liaison. A man of faith, Abraham acted instead in his own imprudence rather than following God's direction. He justified a foolish action through moral relativism, tradition, and human reasoning. He was trying to secure God's blessing on his own terms. It was not until some years later when the son of promise, Isaac, was born that Abraham fully realized the gravity of his mistake. Rejecting the "son of human reasoning," God made a covenant with Isaac, the "son of faith." Ishmael became the father of the Arab race, and Isaac a patriarch of the Hebrews. The Quran teaches that Ishmael, not Isaac, was the son of promise, and that he inherited the land and the title deed to Jerusalem. The battle continues even today.

The United States is caught in the same moral dilemma: wanting to "do good" without God, but only making our halls of government secular, amoral, blind, and impotent. Instead of looking to God for blessings and prosperity, we look to our own reasoning and logic.

We can never win the war on terrorism by appeasing terrorists on the one hand while trying to dislodge them with the other. This is a sure guarantee for another 9/11— or worse. This tide will never be turned without getting to the root of Palestinian hatred for Israel and for the U.S., and exposing its source.

The jihad's "H Bomb" the terrorists' "smart bomb"— is simply Islamic Infidels, human beings, willing to sacrifice their lives for the glory of murdering others. We still cannot accept the fact that the religion of Islamic fundamentalism (Wahhabism and Salafism) can and does kill. These "human" bombs give their lives willingly believing that they will be received into paradise as martyrs because of the corrupt teachings of their leaders. But when they wake up in the afterlife, it won't be God the Father who greets them. They have been deceived, and the consequences are not only gruesome and devastating for those who are left to care for their victims on earth, but will be eternal for the misinformed bombers themselves. The portent of an Islamic "H Bomb" employed by Islamic Infidels is the most ominous sign of a holy war.

Islamic Infidels launched their war in Lebanon when they attacked Israeli forces, the U.S. Marines, and American embassies. The carnage began on April 18, 1983, when a car bomb exploded outside the U.S. Embassy in West Beirut. Sixty-three people died, including 17 Americans. Islamic terrorists gleefully claimed credit for this scurrilous attack. The reason for the attack: Islamic extremists wanted to send a message to the United States to stay clear of Israel. The Muslims claimed that the United States was a pawn of Israel, an assertion that is ludicrous. The brutal attack hammered home this Islamic axiom: *Any friend of Israel is an enemy of ours.* The truth is this: the proxy has always been Israel. She has done more to help the U.S. than all of the Arab countries combined and is the last defense between the "H Bomb" and the West!

America's support for Israel must not waiver. This nation has been blessed because she opened her doors to the Jewish people and has blessed the nation of Israel (Genesis 12:1-3). But America is in danger of moving away from the place of blessing to the place of cursing. The land-for-peace deals of recent years have placed Israel and the Jewish people in grave danger. To weaken Israel is to risk the peace of the world, for the road to world peace will always run through Israel. She is the firewall between America and the anti-Semitic Islamic nations. America's ability to win the war on terrorism is directly related to her willingness to support Israel in the war against Islamic Infidels and their particular brand of terrorism.

8

A NEW ENEMY

The winner of the game [of chess] is the player who makes the next-to-last mistake.[61]

SAVIELLY TARTAKOWER,
POLISH AND FRENCH CHESS MASTER

NO ONE COULD EVER have predicted that the beginning of the twenty-first century would find the United States at war with an enemy devoid of borders, conventional military, and a specific nationality—an enemy with literally no face. This new warfare has proven to be the ultimate chess match with thousands of pawns and all of the kings and queens hidden from view. And, while chess was initially introduced in India, it is the Persians who have been recognized as having perfected and promulgated the brainy game. In the version of chess as played by Iran's leaders, pawns are sent forth to die and take as many people with them as they can, while the world watches wondering where, how, and when the pawns will strike next. The sight of suicide bombers taking out dozens of victims on the buses and in the restaurants of Tel Aviv or Jerusalem was horrible, but the U.S. could still look away. September 11, 2001 changed that—turning fiction into fact, and the unimaginable into reality.

Today, Islamic Infidels have access to chemical and biological weapons that can kill tens of thousands in a matter of minutes. Extremist Islamic terrorist organizations nullify the need to have air power or intercontinental missiles as delivery systems for a nuclear payload. The terrorists themselves are the delivery system, and in the worst of such scenarios, the consequences would be not a car bomb, but a nuclear bomb. With the new threat of thousands—if not millions—dying at a time in the case of terrorists employing chemical, biological, or nuclear weapons, the only logical alternative is to seek out the jihadists before they strike, and then make every effort to eliminate the governments or powers that enable them. Many might think that Iraq was just the first on this list, but when you look at its neighbor, Iran, the battle takes on the ultimate chess-game scenario.

The game began with Iran's opening move—determination to become a nuclear weapons power as quickly as possible. The strategy employed to get to this goal has been both subtle and brilliant.

In order to protect the country's investment in nuclear facilities, Iranian physicists decided it was important to study just how Israel was able to launch a military strike against Iraq's nuclear reactor at *Osirak*. As Professor Louis Rene Beres noted, because of the courage of Prime Minister Menachem Begin in approving an Israeli attack on Iraq's *Osirak* reactor:

> Israel's citizens, together with Jews and Arabs, American, and other coalition soldiers who fought in the [Persian] Gulf War may owe their lives to Israel's courage, skill, and foresight in June 1981. Had it not been for the brilliant raid at *Osirak*, Saddam's forces might have been equipped with atomic warheads in 1991. Ironically, the Saudis, too, are in Jerusalem's debt. Had it not been for Prime Minister Begin's resolve to protect the Israeli people in 1981, Iraq's SCUDs falling on Saudi Arabia might have spawned immense casualties and lethal irradiation.[62]

As a defensive move, Iran's leaders decided to decentralize their nuclear facilities, scattering them around the country. Many such facilities have been embedded in population centers. Thus, to attack successfully Israel or the United States would have to launch a multi-pronged strike which would necessarily be more tactically difficult to plan and implement. Even worse, with nuclear facilities inside Iran's cities, any military strike would cause massive civilian casualties. Would Israel and America be willing to kill thousands of civilians to take out Iran's nuclear facilities in a pre-emptive military attack? Clearly, this would raise the stakes among Israel's enemies.

Iran's leaders further determined that each separate nuclear installation would be devoted to a single purpose, a piece that could be fitted into the puzzle. This way, if a particular facility were attacked and destroyed, Iran would lose only the functions fulfilled at that location. Some operations are being duplicated in other facilities; others might be replaced by outsourcing the fulfillment of the functionality to a friendly country, perhaps to Russia or Pakistan. No successful attack on any one facility could knock offline Iran's total nuclear capabilities for long.

Each step of Iran's nuclear technology has been

designed to allow access to the "full fuel cycle," going from uranium ore to weapons-grade uranium. Since 1988 Iran has opened an estimated ten different uranium mines. Exploration at these sites indicates that the uranium resources of Iran are in the range of 20,000–30,000 tons throughout the country, more than enough to fuel Iran's civilian nuclear power plants well into the future.[63] Obviously, other uses for this fissionable material is intended.

Most nations of the world agree that a freeze on Iran's nuclear program is absolutely necessary for a peaceful Middle East. The halt of production of both highly-enriched uranium and a means to deliver an atomic bomb is essential. Yet, Iran has continued to ignore the warnings of world leaders as well as the International Atomic Energy Agency and the United Nations. As a result, strict sanctions were instituted as a means to end Iranian nuclear pursuits, but those sanctions are now either being eased or withdrawn altogether.

Associated Press correspondent Nasser Karimi indicated on January 12, 2016 that despite reports Iran had begun to disable the Arak reactor, the information was false. Iran's deputy nuclear chief, Ali Asghar Zarean, assured the Iranian people, "Definitely, we will not apply any physical change in this field until a final agreement is finalized."[64] According to Karimi:

> Hard-liners in Iran, who oppose Iranian President Hassan Rouhani and the nuclear deal with world powers, argue that the so-called "disabling" of Arak is a slap in the face of Iran and allegedly evidence of Rouhani having given too many concessions to the West in return [for too little].[65]

The country most vocal about the danger Iran presents to the world is the smallest of nations in its crosshairs—Israel. It is a predicament no twenty-first century nation should have to face—annihilation. Only one member-nation in the United Nations, Israel, has another member, Iran, calling for her to be "wiped off the map." There is little reason to believe it is merely an idle threat as it is so often repeated by Iran's leaders.

An article posted on the Alef website, one with ties to the Iranian supreme leader, calls for the destruction of Jews everywhere:

. . . the opportunity must not be lost to remove "this corrupting material." It is a "'jurisprudential justification" to kill all the Jews and annihilate Israel, and in that, the Islamic government of Iran must take the helm . . . Khamenei announced that Iran will support any nation or group that attacks the "cancerous tumor" of Israel. Though his statement was seen by some in the West as fluff, there is substance behind it . . . The article then quotes the Quran (Albaghara 2:191-193): "And slay them wherever ye find them, and drive them out of the places whence they drove you out, for persecution [of Muslims] is worse than slaughter [of non-believers] . . . and fight them until persecution is no more, and religion is for Allah."[66]

Repeated calls for the destruction of Israel that issued forth from Tehran were at their most vociferous under the leadership of former President Mahmoud Ahmadinejad.

With the advent of a new president in August 2013, the rhetoric was dialed back a bit, but few think Iran's intentions towards the Jewish state have been rescinded. With all the calls today for détente with Iran, only one scripture comes to mind:

> When people are saying, "Everything is peaceful and secure," then disaster will fall on them as suddenly as a pregnant woman's labor pains begin. And there will be no escape.
> (1 Thessalonians 5:3, NLT)

There is little doubt that the desire to destroy Israel is foremost in the minds of Supreme Leader Ali Khamenei and his henchmen as has been proven by the continual supply of arms from Iran to her proxies Syria, Hezbollah in Lebanon and Hamas in Gaza. Rocket attacks launched from both Lebanon and Gaza continue to plague Israeli towns; it is unthinkable for Israel to be faced with the ramifications of a nuclear-armed Iran.

The United States has been very vocal about what is and is not acceptable from Iran but it has been all talk with little, if any, substance. The saber-rattling has been a mere cacophony. The conclusion might very well be that the U.S. is totally intimidated by Iranian oratory. Why would anyone make that assumption? Iran's nuclear program has grown from one centrifuge to as many as 3,000 working to more quickly enrich uranium. This has been accomplished while most world leaders have stood by wringing their collective hands. If the U.S. and Israel fail to take a stand against the threats issued by the supreme ayatollah in charge in Tehran, much more than "face" would be lost.

Even scarier is the thought of how the landscape in the Middle East would be changed if dominated by a nuclear-armed Iran. That notwithstanding, it is one thing to aver that a nuclear-armed Iran is unacceptable and enact sanctions, but quite another to take the steps necessary to stop the achievement of that goal. Thus far, all the grandiloquence has done nothing but cause sniggers behind closed doors in Tehran.

Perhaps the question of greatest import is this: Would the U.S. stand with Israel if it were overtly targeted by Iran? Maybe; maybe not. The difference may be measured by how direct the threat would be to the United States. The time to close the barn door is not after the horses have galloped down the road. The time to stop Iran's nuclear threats is before the first atomic weapon rolls off the assembly line. No one seems to know exactly when that will be, or indeed, whether it has already occurred.

Of greater concern to Israel may be attempts by Iran's current president Hassan Rouhani to persuade the West to further lessen sanctions against his country. Talks in Geneva in November 2013 were aimed at doing just that if concrete changes were made to Iran's nuclear program. Unfortunately, with so much done clandestinely how can anyone be certain of compliance by Iran's rulers?

French leaders were the first to express doubts regarding a long-sought lessening of sanctions in return for a more transparent nuclear program in Iran. According to French Foreign Minister Laurent Fabius, Paris could not agree to a "sucker's deal". As evidence, he pointed to reservations that the Iranians might continue their stealthy march towards securing nuclear arms. The French reticence seemed to indicate that a crack was forming in the Western powers' façade.

Doubts from French leaders were apparently overcome, however, when in November 2013, an interim nuclear deal was struck between Iranian Prime Minister Rouhani and the so-called "P5+1 countries" comprised of the U.S., France, Russia, China, and France plus Germany. The deal gave Iran six months and $7 billion dollars in sanction relief during which time attempts to reach a final agreement on Iran's future nuclear pursuits would be discussed.

Prime Minister Benjamin Netanyahu said at the time:

> What was reached last night in Geneva is not a historic agreement, it is a historic mistake. Today the world became a much more dangerous place because the most dangerous regime in the world made a significant step in obtaining the most dangerous weapons in the world . . . . I want to clarify that Israel will not let Iran develop nuclear military capability.[67]

Leaders of Muslim countries with largely Sunni populations—Saudi Arabia, Kuwait, the United Arab Emirates, Bahrain, Qatar, Egypt and Jordan—were coldly silent on the accord reached in Geneva. Chairman Abdullah al-Askar of Saudi Arabia's Shoura Council, a group that advises the Saudi government on policy said:

> I am afraid Iran will give up

something to get something else from the big powers in terms of regional politics—and I'm worrying about giving Iran more space or a freer hand in the region. The government of Iran, month after month, has proven that it has an ugly agenda in the region, and in this regard no one in the region will sleep and assume things are going smoothly.[68]

Why would Iran's leaders, who have no shortage of insolence and audacity, agree to suspend nuclear enrichment for any period of time? Simple: the money to keep their program running has been severely compromised by the sanctions. There is speculation that what some say could be as much as $100 billion in sanction relief will not benefit the Iranian people, but will go directly into the coffers of Ali Khamenei and the Supreme Leader's Revolutionary Guard Corps. Such a lofty sum would purchase a lot of equipment for the various centrifuges in the land of the ayatollahs.

A U.S. Government Accounting Office (GAO) report released in late February 2016 indicates that the Joint

Comprehensive Plan of Action entered into with Iran may already have cracks that leave its backers in limbo. Such information only seems to corroborate what many in Congress feared. The report stated:

> GAO's preliminary observations indicate that IAEA may face potential challenges in monitoring and verifying Iran's implementation of certain nuclear-related commitments in the JCPOA. According to current and former IAEA and U.S. officials and experts, these potential challenges include (1) integrating JCPOA-related funding into its regular budget and managing human resources in the safeguards program, (2) access challenges depending on Iran's cooperation and the untested JCPOA mechanism to resolve access requests, and (3) the inherent challenge of detecting undeclared nuclear materials and activities—such as potential weapons development activities that may not

involve nuclear material. According to knowledgeable current and former U.S. government officials, detection of undeclared material and activities in Iran and worldwide is IAEA's greatest challenge. According to IAEA documents, Iran has previously failed to declare activity to IAEA.

One thing is certain: If the U.S. hopes to be blessed by God Almighty, her loyalty must be to Israel and not to Israel's enemies; her willingness to act in support of Israel, unwavering. Sadly, the occupant of the White House these days, regardless of party affiliation, seems not to understand that particular biblical precept.

9

ISIS and IRAN

*It's a great huge game of chess that's being played—all
over the world—if this is the world at all, you know.*[69]

L E W I S   C A R R O L L ,
A U T H O R ,   *A L I C E ' S   A D V E N T U R E S   I N   W O N D E R L A N D*

FROM THE MOMENT Ayatollah Ruhollah Khomeini stepped
from the plane onto Iranian soil in 1978 and, then on April
1, 1979, (ironically April Fools' Day) declared his Islamic
Republic he was emboldened and determined to begin
the spread of fanatical Islam using a network of terrorist
organizations. Khomeini's vicious voice fiercely advocating
violence impregnated the entire Middle East with Islamic
Infidels who gladly chose the path of hatred and destruction. His offspring have become more radicalized than he
might ever have dreamed.

According to the U.S. Council for Foreign Relations, today Iran supports such proxy groups as Hamas and Palestinian Islamic Jihad[70]; and Brookings Institution reports that another sub-contractor, Hezbollah in Lebanon, has been responsible for killing more Americans than any other single global terrorist group.[71]

The global reach of the Carter administration-blessed Khomeini was not restricted to Iran. In a treatise by Gen. (Ret.) Moshe Ya'alon, he wrote:

> According to Iranian Supreme Leader Ali Khamenehi and Iran's Syrian partners, the Second Lebanon War [August 2006] was launched by Hezbollah—Iran's proxy—as a hostile probe of U.S. reflexes via the engagement of Israel, which for Iran and Syria is a direct extension of Washington in the Middle East.[72]

It is apparent that Tehran wishes to neutralize America's influence in the Middle East as a major step in the plan to defeat Western civilization. Foremost in that effort has been the funding, training, and arming of Hezbollah in Lebanon, and not just with pistols, rockets and ammunition.

Iran directly supports its chosen groups of Islamic Infidels such as Hezbollah and Hamas with funds and training. For years Lebanon has played host to about 250 members of the Islamic Revolutionary Guard Corps, the elite of the Iranian military, that is best at training other terror units. It is obvious to me that Iran has a long-term plan to take control of the Middle East region by using proxies: Hamas, Hezbollah, and Palestinian Islamic Jihad, and its own Revolutionary Guard. Would the spread of such terrorist entities have been assured had Jimmy Carter worked with the shah to correct human rights issues rather than against the monarch culminating in his overthrow and expulsion from Iran?

Page after page could be filled with terror attacks that have implicated Iran or Iranian proxies since the taking of the American hostages in 1979. Below are just a few instances:

✦ Iran's proxies have attempted to infiltrate and/or smuggle arms and explosives into France, Germany, Saudi Arabia, Tunisia, and Turkey, to name a few.

✦ Kidnappings and murders:

William Buckley, American, kidnapped and murdered by Iran's Revolutionary Guards; Peter Kilburn, librarian, American University, Beirut, kidnapped and murdered; Michel Seurat, French writer, kidnapped and murdered by hostage-takers; Colonel William Higgins, American officer assigned to the U.N. in Lebanon, kidnapped and executed by Iranian agents; Professor Hitoshi Igarashi, Japanese translator of Salman Rushdie's *Satanic Verses,* stabbed to death; Ettore Capriolo, Italian translator, survived being stabbed; William Nygaard, the Norwegian publisher of Rushdie's book, barely survived an assassination attempt in Oslo in 1993; Hikmet Cettin, a Turkish journalist, murdered.

✧ Iran has been linked to bombings worldwide:

1983—U.S. Embassy in Beirut (sixty-one killed, 120 injured); U.S. Marine headquarters in Beirut (241 killed, 80 seriously injured); series of Paris bombings in 1986; 1989 bombings in Mecca (scores injured); Amia Jewish Center, Buenos Aires (95 killed, 230 injured); 1996 bombing outside the Khobar Towers in Saudi Arabia (20 murdered, nearly 400 wounded).

✧ Hijackings and airline explosions:

1983—Air France 747—plane destroyed at Tehran's Mehrabad Airport.

1985—TWA Boeing 727—U.S. Navy diver Robert Dean Stethem severely beaten and later executed by hijackers.

1987—Air Afrique DC-10—French passenger murdered.

1988—Kuwaiti 747—landed at

Mashhad, Iran; two passengers murdered.

1988—Pan Am Flight 103 exploded in midair over Lockerbie, Scotland, 270 passengers from 21 countries perished.[73]

✧ Iran and 9/11—The 9/11 Commission report linked Iran to at least facilitating the travel plans of the 9/11 terrorist/murderers by not stamping their passports.[74] There was also evidence that Iran assisted al-Qaeda when that organization was forced to withdraw from Afghanistan in 2001 and has, in fact, allowed that rogue group to continue to operate from within Iran's borders.

✧ October 7, 2000—Hezbollah operatives abducted an Israeli businessman and three Israeli soldiers patrolling Israel's border with Lebanon. The soldiers' remains and the businessman were returned to Israel in 2004.

✧ March 12, 2002—Shooting attack against Israeli vehicles near the

Israeli-Lebanese border: six were killed, seven injured.

✧ July 12, 2006—Hezbollah operatives killed eight Israeli soldiers and kidnapped two others stationed in Israeli sovereign territory. The soldiers' remains were returned to Israel in July 2008. May 2011—Hezbollah targeted the Israeli consul to Turkey, Moshe Kimchi, in a bombing that injured eight Turkish citizens.

✧ July 2012—A Hezbollah suicide bomber attacked the tour bus of a group of Israelis in Burgas, Bulgaria. Five members of the Israeli group were murdered as was the bus driver.

The world saw Iran's true intentions on January 4, 2002, the day Israelis intercepted a Palestinian ship, the *Karine-A*, in the Red Sea. The ship was loaded with Katyusha rockets which have a maximum range of twelve miles as well as assault rifles, antitank missiles, mines, ammunition, and explosives. Most of the weapons were Iranian, and all were bound for Iran's proxies entrenched in Gaza and Lebanon.

Make no mistake; Iran poses a grave nuclear threat, not only to the region, but to the world. Peaceful Muslims worldwide are slowly being hijacked by the more radical Islamic Infidels. Its leaders have positioned Iran as a central player in the Shi'ite versus Sunni sects of Islam. They rejoiced when the U.S. Embassy in Tehran was overrun and Americans held hostage for 444 days. The jubilation continued when Iranian proxies in Lebanon struck a deadly blow to the aforementioned Marine compound that resulted in the U.S. packing its bags and going home. Iran focused on Iraq with every intention of driving coalition troops out of that country just as it did in Lebanon, thus creating a unified Shia state from the Persian Gulf to the borders of Syria, and eventually, beyond. Meanwhile, to the west, Israel stands by watching quietly and preparing to defend herself against any and all threats.

The danger that emanates from Iran's proxies—Hezbollah, Hamas, and Islamic Jihad—is the direct result of the overarching belief that each terrorist entity speaks for Allah and is acting at his behest to bring death to those who oppose them.

Iran is the center of gravity for the Islamic Infidel wolf pack. Its footprint can be seen in comments made by the head of Hezbollah, Hassan Nasrallah, who refers to

himself as the special envoy of Iran's supreme leader, Ali
Khamenei. This gives subtle overtones of Shia radicalism
to Hezbollah. Incredibly, at last count the terrorist group
had some 50,000 rockets aimed toward Israel. And while
the Islamic Jihad terrorists in Gaza with their 5,000
rockets can't vie in numbers, they can compete in the
intensity of their hatred for the Jewish nation.

There was a time when Arab pawns were charac-
terized by the country from which they came (nationalism.) Today they more readily identify themselves
simply as practicing or non-practicing Muslims. The fac-
tors that will one day blur the lines dividing the Shi'ite
and the Sunni Muslims is their hatred for Israel and
a desire of both to see an Islamic caliphate dominate
the world.

If the United States relinquishes its role as leader of
the free world, and allows Iran to pursue its nuclear ambi-
tions to a logical conclusion, the world will have changed
forever. The Nuclear Non-Proliferation Treaty will not be
worth the paper on which it was written. Several Middle
East countries, including Egypt, have already determined
to follow the nuclear path if Iran is successful. Some will
simply acquire nuclear weapons without fanfare. The U.S.
and its allies will be impotent to corral the resulting chaos.

It will be like trying to gather in the midst of a *haboob*, a hot desert wind.

A nuclear arms race between the Shi'ites and Sunnis who occupy the 200-mile Persian Gulf coast all but guarantees a coming Armageddon. Countries that cannot afford to enter the nuclear race will be obliged or coerced to take sides, and many will side with the bully on the block which produces a plethora of Islamic Infidels—Iran.

Since her rebirth Israel has been a staunch ally of the United States and a bastion of democracy in the region. The U.S. must not turn its back on Israel as it has on Egypt, Yemen, and other Middle East allies in the throes of change. *The Atlantic Times* reports that Israeli terrorism expert Boaz Ganor, head of the International Policy Institute for Counter-Terrorism, believes "the U.S. made a wrong judgment call by turning her back on the ousted President Hosni Mubarak, and 'sending the disastrous message that allies cannot rely on the USA.' . . . Ganor believes that without [Mubarak] the U.S. is 'much weaker today . . . "[75]

The strong military deterrence provided by the tiny nation of Israel is of the utmost importance in pursuing peace in the Middle East. Thus far it has been only preventative because Israel has not been allowed to unleash the might of her military arsenal against her enemies. At some point, however, the line of demarcation will be crossed and Israel will be forced to do what its allies do not seem to have the courage to do. (Remember Iraq's *Osirik* nuclear reactor that was destroyed by the Israelis in a surprise air attack June 1981?) If the U.S. fails to stand behind Israel's attempts to free the world from Iran's implied threats of nuclear attack, the results will be catastrophic.

On the other hand, if the U.S. stiffens its resolve to be the true leader of the Western world and actively takes its place as such, the threat from Iran will be averted and the countries now seeking democracy and a better way of life will not be held hostage by religious radicals who wish to control not only the Middle East but the world.

While it would be folly to predict how the turmoil in the Middle East will play out, it is obvious that the country benefiting most in the long run will be Iran, its radical mullahs and its cadre of Islamic Infidels. In the meantime, we must become better educated about the enemies we face and what strategies will be effective to defeat them.

Another terror organization in the Middle East is Palestinian Islamic Jihad (PIJ). It is linked closely to the Muslim Brotherhood. As with its counterparts Hamas and Hezbollah, it, too, is committed to the destruction of the nation of Israel. Its focus is not on social programs to better the welfare of the Palestinian people, but only on jihad. PIJ aims for devastating assaults against the Jewish people—in both the military and civilian quarters. These Islamic Infidels deploy both women and children in their brutal attacks.

According to sources compiled by the Jewish Virtual Library:

> PIJ attacks from 2005 through 2013 have been primarily rocket attacks aimed at southern Israeli cities, but have also included attacking Israeli targets with explosive devices, especially military patrols along the Israel-Gaza border. The US Department of State believes PIJ's strength to be less than 1,000 members though it receives complete financial assistance and military training from Iran.[76] [77]

In the game of chess there is a move called a "positional sacrifice." Any piece can be positioned for surrender, but more commonly it is the pawn. Iran's proxies have been positioned to become the pawns in its horrendous game to destroy both Israel and the United States. Each group is expendable as long as its sacrifice moves the chess master closer to his objective—a crushing win against the opponent.

10

PROXIES AT WAR

My greatest fear is the Iranians acquire a nuclear
weapon and give it to a terrorist organization.
And there is a real threat of them doing that.

SENATOR JOHN MCCAIN

MY BOOK *Beyond Iraq, the Final Move* was a treatise based
on the war in Iraq—a proxy war between Iran and the United
States. The U.S. had sent troops into Iraq to unseat Saddam
Hussein based on information regarding the dictator's cache
of chemical weapons. Iran once again employed its chess
strategy and backed yet another proxy, Shi'ite leader Sheik
Muqtada al-Sadr and his Mahdi Army. With the rise of the
Islamic State in Iraq and Syria, the burning question that
no one has yet posited, but one which demands an answer
is this: Is this latest derivative of terrorism a clandestine
proxy of Iran?

In July 2014 an al Qaeda splinter group seized some of Iraq's largest cities and marched toward Baghdad with thousands of well-armed jihadists. Their goal: the creation of an Islamic state. The group is sometimes called ISIL, or the Islamic State of the Levant (a large area in the Middle East bordered by the Mediterranean, the Arabian Desert, and Upper Mesopotamia)—meaning the terrorist group ultimately has designs on the entire region.

On September 29, 2014, Israeli Prime Minister Benjamin Netanyahu stood before the United Nations General Assembly and issued a grave warning to those assembled:

> Because everywhere we look, militant Islam is on the march . . . . Typically, its first victims are other Muslims, but it spares no one.
>
> Christians, Jews, Yazidis, Kurds— no creed, no faith, no ethnic group is beyond its sights. And it's rapidly spreading in every part of the world . . . . For the militant Islamists, "All politics is global." Because their

ultimate goal is to dominate the world . . . .

ISIS and Hamas are branches of the same poisonous tree. ISIS and Hamas share a fanatical creed, which they both seek to impose well beyond the territory under their control.

Listen to ISIS's self-declared caliph, Abu Bakr Al-Baghdadi. This is what he said two months ago: "A day will soon come when the Muslim will walk everywhere as a master . . . The Muslims will cause the world to hear and understand the meaning of terrorism . . . and destroy the idol of democracy" . . . . The Middle East is in chaos. States are disintegrating. Militant Islamists are filling the void.[78]

As Mr. Netanyahu reminded the world, an unrestrained Islamic revolution populated by Islamic Infidels is spreading from Iran through Iraq, Syria, Lebanon, and the Palestinian territory and threatens the border with Turkey, all while the world sleeps. The goal is to take over the Middle East and ultimately the entire world. Many of us don't understand the true nature of what it will take to defeat this global web of terror. At the time, we didn't seem to realize that Iraq was not a war in itself, but only one of the initial battles in the overall war on terrorism. Too many didn't recognize that the next World War had already begun and we are right in the middle of it. We must not fall prey to that mindset again.

Through all the acronyms and name transformations, IS has maintained its original footprint: horrific acts of terror designed to spread fear and revulsion. The ravening beasts smell blood and are on the hunt with the intent to destroy the world as we know it. This again proved to be true when a letter was publicly posted on the doors of various Swedish towns, including Stockholm, the capital city, threatening its citizens with beheading if they did not immediately convert to Islam.

The flyers stated simply but graphically:

> In the name of Allah, the merciful, full of grace. You who are not believ- ers will be decapitated in three days in your own house. We will bomb your rotten corpses afterwards. You

must choose between these three choices: 1. Convert to Islam. 2. Pay the jizya [religious tax] for protection. 3. Or else, you will be decapitated. The police will not prevent or save you from you being murdered. (Death comes to all of you).[79]

James Wright Foley, a thirty-year-old journalist, was beheaded in August 2014, the first American to face such heinous execution at the hands of ISIL. His death was followed in September by that of Steven Joel Sotloff, also a victim of beheading. A forty-seven-year-old British aid worker, Alan Henning, and a French tourist and mountaineering guide, Herve Gourdel, were then beheaded by ISIL terrorists. A third U.S. hostage, Peter Kassig, was beheaded by his ISIL captors in November 2014. Kayla Mueller was captured by ISIS operatives while working with Doctors without Borders. She was reportedly killed when the building in which she was held was bombed.

In a joyfully released press statement following the November 2015 Paris massacre that left 130 dead, IS celebrated its victory over the city it called, "The lead carrier of the cross." The group declared, "Allah granted victory upon their hands and cast terror into the hearts of the crusaders in their very own homeland."[80]

The December 2015 attack in San Bernardino, California was the deadliest on U.S. soil since 9/11. A self-radicalized couple, Tashfeen Malik and her husband, Syed Rizwan Farook, killed 14 and injured 21 others in the deadly melee. Days later, the FBI announced that it had labeled the incident an "act of terrorism." While the Islamic State hailed the two as "martyrs" and "supporters" it failed to claim responsibility for the assault.

Great darkness surrounds the West and the Middle East. Everywhere embedded Islamic Infidels pledging allegiance to IS are watching and waiting for the opportunity to spring into action and take the lives of one, hundreds or even thousands; it matters not to them. Even a single instance of terror—a single death—brings the desired result: fear.

Perhaps we should take note of Franklin D. Roosevelt's March 4, 1933 Inaugural address in which he challenged:

> So first of all let me assert my
> firm belief that the only thing we
> have to fear is fear itself—name-
> less, unreasoning, unjustified terror

which paralyzes the needed effort to
bring about needed efforts to convert
retreat into advance.[81]

Sadly, the incursion of IS into Syria has threatened
Iran proxy Bashar al Assad and given his friends in
Moscow the perfect rationale to rush to Assad's aid and
assure that he remains in power. A U.S. official in Iraq,
Ali Khedery, surmises that Russia's leader has an ulte-
rior motive. Khedery believes President Vladimir Putin's
move indicates a "fundamental shifting of the balance of
power in the Middle East . . . . and will have key global
consequences. Khedery also suggests:

> There is now a Shia axis locked in
> combat across Iraq, Syria, and Yemen
> . . . . This has the potential to escalate
> into a regional war, a holy war, and
> global cold war.[82]

Another reason the Russians may have used the
IS threat to sprint to Assad's aide is because Syria has a
number of warm water ports; something in short supply
for Putin. Russia currently leases facilities at Tartus,
Syria, as a base for repairing and resupplying Russian

warships. Lack of support for Assad could cost Putin this port in a storm.

In his address to the UN in late September 2015, Putin attacked the U.S. for having created a void into which terrorists such as ISIS have poured. He apparently has little fear that President Barack Obama will, in the waning days of his presidency, jump into the fray against Assad and bolster U.S.- backed rebels in the region. Putin's gambit at the UN only served to make the Obama administration weaker and even less effective that it has been until now.

The winner in this face-off will likely be the Islamic Infidels who will use this latest Russian escalation as nothing more than another recruiting tool to draw jihadists into the region. Rather than ending the civil war in Syria, the move will likely only prolong, and perhaps escalate, what has always been an untenable conflict.

Under cover of targeting ISIS command posts in the region, Russian Sukhoi-34, Sukhoi-24M and Sukhoi-25 warplanes have flown numerous sorties over Syria. Sadly, and although Russia claims to have hit five ISIS targets in Syria, the attacks also led to the bombing of groups opposed to Assad. After several days of denying having hit non-ISIS targets Putin finally acknowledged the error.[83]

The Russian forays into Syria will almost certainly lead to retaliation from Islamic Infidels who will flock to fight a new faction of atheists and infidels who have targeted them. The risks for Putin may well outweigh the rewards if he finds himself a target for jihadists bent on his destruction. The Bear may well have wished it had stayed in hibernation rather than dip into the beehive that is the fanatical Islamist Middle East.

This all presents difficult problems for a cash-strapped Russian economy. How long will Putin be able to sustain his backing of Assad with weapons and warplanes? Will his decision lead to another Afghanistan quagmire? How long can his forces survive before being compelled to turn tail and rush back to Russia?

With the Russian incursion, yet another dilemma arises: Putin has only a small hope of defeating ISIS with the support of Sunni Muslims—fundamentally, Saudi Arabia. That has little chance of happening, as the Russians are backing the Shia in Iran.

The predominant question in many minds is: What exactly is Putin's end game in the Middle East? Journalist Neil MacFarquhar of the *New York Times* addressed the possibilities:

The partial truce that Russia and the United States have thrashed out in Syria capped something of a foreign policy trifecta for President Vladimir V. Putin, with the Kremlin strong-arming itself into a pivotal role in the Middle East, Ukraine floundering and the European Union developing cracks like a badly glazed pot . . . . In Syria, Russia achieved its main goal of shoring up the government of President Bashar al-Assad, long the Kremlin's foremost Arab ally. Yet its ultimate objectives remain murky, not least navigating a graceful exit from the messy conflict . . . .

Even as the Syrian government and a major opposition group said on Tuesday that they would observe a conditional pause in the fighting, there remains a gaping loophole in the agreement in that it permits attacks against the Islamic State and the Nusra Front, an Al Qaeda affiliate, to continue. This could work in Moscow's favor, since many of the anti-Assad groups aligned with the United States fight alongside the Nusra Front.

Thus, while American allies are being asked to stop fighting Mr. Assad's government, Russia and the Syrian government can continue to strike United States-backed rebel groups without fear, if history is any guide, of Washington's doing anything to stop them.[84]

Israel, too, is faced with a new quandary: How does it fight terror at its borders without a head-to-head confrontation with Russia?

And Israel isn't the only nation in the region that could be caught in the maelstrom. This latest move by Putin could mean dire consequences for Jordan. That small country has taken in approximately 630,000 Syrian refugees. In 1970 Jordan experienced the threat of a revolution when the PLO tried to overthrow King Hussein, only to be thwarted and driven from Jordan. Terrorist

Abu Musab al Zarqawi was Jordanian-born, but learned his trade under Osama bin Laden.

The world seems ripe for a perfect storm with America's president and Vladimir Putin possibly facing off in Syria. U.S. allies also have a stake in this fight. The coalition backing rebels in Syria has called for the Russian Federation to end bombing runs in Syria. A coalition spokesperson has expressed grave reservations "with regard to the Russian military build-up in Syria and especially attacks . . . on Hama, Homs and Idlib . . . which led to civilian casualties and did not target [ISIL]."[85]

While the world ponders a possible encounter between the Russian Bear and the American Eagle in Syria, Islamic Infidels bearing the IS flag creep closer to Israel. In January 2015, a group linked to the Islamic State attacked Egyptian security forces in the Sinai Peninsula and cost the lives of dozens of Egypt's military. It was the largest battle in the region since the *Yom Kippur* War in 1973. The Islamic State attacked on fifteen different fronts and caught the Egyptians completely off-guard. Also a major concern was that the assaults took advantage of modern weapons no outsider knew were available to the Islamic State. Although these forays were against Egypt, it would be just as simple for ISIL Islamic Infidels to launch rocket and mortar attacks against Israel.

Egypt responded by contacting Israel's government for permission to move F-16 fighter jets and Apache helicopters into the desert, and the Israeli Air Force flew additional missions along the border. Both Egyptian and Israeli leaders are well aware that the Islamic State might use provocative, targeted attacks against Israel to cause renewed tension between their two countries.

Today, Iran's proxies are encircling the Jewish state—Hezbollah in Lebanon and Hamas in Gaza, just waiting for an opportunity to strike. ISIL, another deadly threat, has made inroads into Syria and the Sinai. Sadly, in the midst of threatening times, Israel's friends are too often walking away—leaving her isolated and alone just as she faces her most dangerous threats. The entire region is on the brink of war . . . . war that could very quickly become the most bloody and devastating in decades. The liberal media does its best to downplay the role of radical Islam in this crisis. President Obama has even gone so far as to say that the Islamic State terrorist group (ISIL) is not really Islamic[86] . . . but it is. It's a ragtag band of Islamic Infidels completely devoid of conscience.

11

PROPHECY
FULFILLED

So when the last and dreadful hour
This crumbling pageant shall devour,
The trumpet shall be heard on high,
The dead shall live, the living die,
And Music shall untune the sky.[87]

JOHN DRYDEN,
ENGLISH POET AND PLAYWRIGHT

THE WORLD'S SPOTLIGHT is and has been on Iran for decades—since the arrival of Ayatollah Ruhollah Khomeini and his band of Islamic Infidels bent on destroying the United States and Israel. With the implementation of proxy wars to fulfill that aim, it has been difficult sometimes to identify the players.

With Iran ready to act as mother hen and gather multiple fledgling proxies under her wing, the stage is set for a dangerous, eerie new alliance in the Middle East. I believe the long-term plan of these Islamic Infidels is to establish a Sunni caliphate in the most advantageous locale. Is that where we are heading while America sits idly by with its wrists bound by the whims of the United Nations? It now seems that the U.S. administration will do little without the approval of that august body. The eventual damage done globally by fumbling the situations in Syria, Yemen, Iraq and other Arab countries will be just as great as was that in Iran.

As if all of that were not chilling enough, the realignment of the loyalties in the Middle East brings an even more foreboding threat. In the changing face of that part of the world, are we seeing the beginning of the Russian/ Iranian-led coalition of nations foretold in the Scriptures? Is this the birth of the army of nations unified against Israel as revealed in Ezekiel 38 and 39, and the initial teetering of the next domino of Bible prophecy? Looking at the current line-up of players, it is becoming harder and harder to deny the words of Ezekiel in chapters 38 and 39 regarding Gog and Magog and the coming Armageddon (the last battle between good and evil, between God and Satan.)

The two "princes" of Persia and Greece appear to be fallen angels who delayed the heavenly being that came to Daniel with a word from God during his twenty-one days of fasting. Since Gog is mentioned twice in Scripture—in Ezekiel 38-39 and again in Revelation 20, which describes what will take place at the end of the Millennium—it seems likely Gog may not be a nation or a person but an anti-Semitic, antichrist spirit that stirs up hatred against God's people and probably has done so for many centuries. This may be the same spirit that was behind the events beginning in Daniel 11:36, behind such men as Nero and Hitler, and those who will aid the Antichrist in his fight to destroy the Jews once and for all during the second half of the Tribulation.

Though the exact nature of Gog may be uncertain, the names Magog, Tubal, and Meshech point to the regions settled by the sons of Japheth, the third son of Noah (see Genesis 10:2 and 1 Chronicles 1:1-27). These three were grandsons of Noah who, according to tradition, settled their families in the lands north of the Black and Caspian Seas. Traditionally, the trio combined to represent the nation of Russia, with Meshech being the father of the settlement that came to be Moscow and Tubal the founder of the city of Tobolsk.

Tobolsk is north of Kazakhstan and Pakistan, on the western edge of the West Siberian Plain, about two hundred miles from the eastern foothills of the Ural Mountains. If you draw a line north and south through Tobolsk, the land west of that is home to the largest percentage of a Russian populace, even though it occupies only about a third of the country. Tobolsk has a population of less than 100,000. It takes its name from the Tobol River, which flows north and slightly east from the southern end of the Urals. The city sits at the point where the Tobol flows into the Irtysh River, and from there it merges with the Ob and ultimately empties into the Arctic Ocean. The town is about 500 miles from the northernmost point of the Caspian Sea. I believe, as do many scholars, that Tobol derives its name directly from Noah's grandson, Tubal. This makes even more sense when you remember that Hebrew is an alphabet of consonants only, making Tobol and Tubal literally the same word.

The origin of Russia is a phenomenal, prophetic journey. Because of its size, it encountered constant tension on all sides: Asia, Europe, the Vikings, and the Slavs. That Russia's ancestors emerged from the sons of Noah has long been recognized, even by such men as the French philosopher Voltaire, who wrote in *The Philosophical*

Dictionary, "There is a genealogical tree of the events in this world. It is incontestable that . . . the Russians [descended] from Magog . . . one finds this genealogy in so many fat books!"[88]

The origin of the Slavs is a complete mystery to historians; it is not even enshrouded in legend. It is likely they were farmers in the Black Sea region before the Scythian invasions that took place around 700 BC. The earliest signs of nationalism in the region were south of Kiev (where my great grandfather was born), which seems to indicate these tribes were originally moving south to north. However, it wasn't until the ninth century AD, when the Vikings invaded, that the focal point of Russian culture moved up to Moscow.

Because of this and other research we don't have space enough to include here, there is little debate among scholars of Bible prophecy that Magog, Tubal, and Meshech point to Russia as the lead nation of this coalition. This is now believed to be true even though for centuries it seemed impossible.

When Cyrus Scofield published his famous study Bible in 1909, he included in his notes on Ezekiel 38 and 39 that Russia would invade Israel in the end-times. At the time, that interpretation was challenged and even mocked. Many said, "How can you possibly say that? Russia is a Christian Orthodox nation, and Israel doesn't even exist . . . nor is there any possibility that Israel will exist." Scofield answered simply, "I don't understand it, and I can't explain it, but the Bible says it, and I believe it."[89]

Today no one doubts that Russia might attack Israel—even unbelievers—especially since Russia has been known to regularly place Israeli cities in the crosshairs of its nuclear missiles. It once stockpiled roughly $2 billion worth of weapons and equipment in southern Lebanon, which the Israeli army uncovered in a network of caves in 1982. Today Scofield's interpretation is generally taken for granted among prophetic circles, even though for centuries it had seemed ridiculous.

The shift in Russian regard for a Jewish state was to be followed by another occurrence that would have seemed impossible at the turn of the last century. Today, the strongest ally of Russia in the Middle East is undoubtedly Iran, the nation listed in Ezekiel as "Persia." The fact that Iran is modern-day Persia is certain. Its name was changed from "Persia" to "Iran" in 1935—and *Ērān* is actually the Middle Persian pronunciation of the name for the country. In 1971, the shah of Iran held an enormous festival (costing an estimated $200 million) at the foot of the ruins of Persepolis[90] in southern Iran to commemorate the 2,500[th] anniversary of the Persian Empire, whose birth is dated to the same year Daniel had his vision of the Seventy Weeks.

Oddly enough, in the history of the world the last two decades represent the only time that Russia and Persia have been anywhere close to hospitable to each other. The two nations were almost continuously at war from 1722 to 1828. During that time Persia fought a war of attrition with Russia and Great Britain but never lost its independence as other nations in the region did, although it did lose a great deal of territory.

In 1925 Reza Khan overthrew the weakening Qajar Dynasty and proclaimed himself the first "shah." He tried to model Persia after western industrialized nations, but because of its close ties with Germany at the time, Iran was again attacked by Russia and Great Britain in 1941. These Allied powers badly needed Iran's railroads to transport their war materiel. Following World War II, Iran remained closely tied to Great Britain and nearly became a constitutional democracy in the early 1950s. This, however, was thwarted by the United States and Great Britain in Operation Ajax, because the parliament in London wanted to wrest control of Iran's oil fields from British Petroleum.[91] Because of Operation Ajax, Iran's parliament was disbanded and the shah became a dictator. This would be the West's greatest blunder in the Middle East until Jimmy Carter allowed the shah to be deposed during the Islamic Revolution of 1979.[92] Until then, Iran had been a steadfast Western ally, armed by the United States to be the fifth most powerful military in the world.

After the fall of the shah, Iran was so embroiled in its war with Iraq from 1980 to 1988 that it had little time or energy for foreign relations. Considering all of this, the fact that Russia and Iran are now such close political bedfellows is unprecedented. This is the only time the world has ever seen cooperation, let alone open relations, between the two empires that had been bitter enemies for centuries.

Cush and Put—as mentioned in Ezekiel 38:5—were sons of Ham, Noah's second son. According to Genesis 10, they traveled south into Northern Africa from the Ark's final resting place on Mount Ararat (Mount Ararat sits at the eastern edge of Turkey, against Turkey's borders with Iran and Armenia). Most scholars believe these two names represent at least the North African nations of Sudan, Libya, and Ethiopia.

Sudan voted to divide into two nations, a Muslim/
Arab north and a Christian/African south. This was finalized on July 9, 2011. The Arab north—the nation was home
to the birth of Al-Qaeda—would undoubtedly have no
love for Israel. Not only that, but the Sudan has its own
interesting history dealing with Muhammad Ahmad bin
Abd Allah, the self-proclaimed "Mahdi," who chased the
British from the region in the 1880s.[93]

Put's descendants populated the area west of Egypt,
so today we would equate Put with the nations of modern
Libya, Algeria, Tunisia, and Morocco, which are Islamic
states. As we have already discussed, rioting and violence
recently toppled Tunisia's government, and its immediate
future is unclear. Egypt stands at a similar crossroads,
and the civil war in Libya saw General Muammar Gaddafi
ousted and killed, but has as yet produced no clear-cut new
leader. At the outset of hostilities there, Russia, Germany,
and China initially stood with Gaddafi when the U.N. proposed a no-fly zone over the country to limit his attacks on
the rebels. They later abstained when the vote for a no-fly
zone was finally passed, and they subsequently refused to
take part in enforcing it.

The last two on the list, Gomer and Beth-togarmah,
are also mentioned in Genesis 10. Gomer was the eldest son

of Japheth who, as we mentioned previously, was also the father of Magog, Tubal, and Meshesh. Togarmah—*Beth-togarmah* means "house of Togarmah"—was Gomer's third and last son. Gomer's descendants were called *Gi-mir-ra-a*, which the Greeks translated as "Cimmerians." A fair amount of ancient information exists regarding these Indo-European nomads, who were eventually driven out of Asia Minor northward through the Caucasus region (today the nations of Georgia, Azerbaijan, and Armenia) and into the steppes of southern Russia. They, like the descendants of Meshech, may have formed another central core of the Slavic race or, as some believe, were driven west to become eastern Europeans or Germans.

The Assyrians called *Beth-togarmah* "Til-garimmu," a name derived from the Hittite *Tegarama* and carried into classical times as *Gauraena*, or the town of *Gürün* in Turkey today. The Assyrians destroyed *Gauraena* in 695 BC. Because they were known for breeding and trading horses and mules in ancient times—*"From Beth-togarmah they exchanged horses, war horses, and mules for your wares"* (Ezekiel 27:14)—it is customary to associate the descendants of Beth-togarmah with the Cossacks of the Ukraine in southern Russia, who have long been world-famous horsemen.

A long-time ally of Israel, Turkey has slowly decreased its ties with the Jewish state. Tensions between Ankara and Jerusalem continue to grow while Turkish Prime Minister Recep Erdogan openly courted Iran and welcomed the Islamization of his country. His move to join Brazil in an alliance with Iran, attempting to forestall further sanctions against Mahmoud Ahmadinejad's regime, was just one more link in the chain toward Islamic domination in Turkey.

The Turkish government expelled the Israeli ambassador and suspended all military agreements with Israel, demanding Israel's apology for intercepting the anti-Israel, "Free Gaza" flotilla launched from Turkey—even though it was backed by a Turkish terrorist organization. Of course, Hamas and the Arab world applauded Turkey's move against the Jewish nation.

Israeli Ambassador to the U.S. Michael Oren had been hopeful that Israel and Turkey would retain a relationship based on mutual respect:

> Our policy has not changed but Turkey's policy has changed, very much, over the last few years. Under a different government with an Islamic

orientation, Turkey has turned away from the West. We certainly do not have any desire in any further deterioration in our relations with the Turks. It's an important Middle Eastern power. It has been a friend in the past.[94]

Enmity between Israel and Turkey has been ongoing although as of this writing diplomatic discussions on restoring normal relations continue.

In late 2015, Israeli and Turkish officials met in an attempt to restore the fractured alliance. While there is some hope of détente, Israel remains skeptical due to Turkish support of Hamas and reports of Turkey buying ISIS-controled oil. Only time will tell if or when the rift is mended.

12

RUSSIA and CHINA:
THE BEAR and the DRAGON

I think ISIS is very dangerous indeed . . . Especially
if you think about the prospects of nuclear
weapons being developed in the Middle East.[95]

FORMER VICE PRESIDENT DICK CHENEY

THE BOOK OF EZEKIEL gives us a view of some of the trading partners that might be brought under the umbrella of Russia's allies. Sheba, Dedan, and Tarshish are mentioned as partners with Tyre, as are some of the other allies of Gog. (See Ezekiel 27) If this is the case, then all of them must have been within caravan or sailing distance of Tyre, which is in the southern part of modern-day Lebanon. Looking at maps of ancient times, Dedan would be in modern-day Saudi Arabia, Sheba in or near Yemen, and Tarshish is often considered to have been a European port in Spain or England. If that were true, then the *"merchants of Tarshish"* would likely refer to a trading alliance or economic union of western or European countries. While some have tried to stretch this to include the United States as part of its *"villages"* or colonies, this seems unlikely, though there is no way of knowing for certain.

If we accept this premise, and a Russian/Iranian coalition of proxies were to attack Israel, Saudi Arabia and the other states of the Arabian Peninsula—Jordan, Yemen, Oman, Qatar, Bahrain, The United Arab Emirates, Kuwait, and even Iraq (which are largely Sunni Muslim nations and are more friendly with the West)—would be unlikely to participate in any attack on Israel. As a group, they and the West would be in a position to question the Russo-Iranian coalition's motives and actions. If the European Economic Union and/or the West as a whole were part of the opposition as the *"merchants of Tarshish with all its villages,"*[96] it seems more likely it would resemble the ineffectual initial protests following the late Gaddafi's attacks against his own people in Libya. Either way, as the rest of Ezekiel 38 and 39 plays out, there isn't really enough time for Dedan, Sheba, and those of Tarshish to get involved in the skirmish before it will already be over.

Those condemned by God in the initial verses of Ezekiel 38 for attacking Israel are a coalition of Russia, Iran, Northern African Islamic states, and perhaps Turkey. To add a modern update, they would likely also include Iran's proxies—Hezbollah and Hamas—and the countries they occupy—Lebanon, Syria, and the Gaza Strip. As I write this, the continuing Syrian civil war could change the face of that nation, and perhaps that of Jordan as well, especially with the influx of refugees.

In looking at which nations would probably be part of this coalition, it is important to note that Ezekiel was identifying people groups as opposed to regions or countries. Subsequent migrations of these clans could easily make the anti-Israel coalition described here of a slightly different make-up. For example, it could also include some of the old Soviet satellite countries, other Islamic states, or even some European countries such as Germany, where some believe the descendants of Gomer ultimately settled. The bottom line is that with Russia's current alliance with Iran to develop its nuclear program and Iran's pledge to "wipe Israel off the face of the Earth," it is not difficult to see the two nations as architects of an attack to once and for all destroy Israel.

In recent years China and Russia have formed what

might be loosely described as a protectorate for Iran. This tripartite back-burner agreement has proven to be reciprocally advantageous for all. Steve Schippert, co-founder of the Center for Threat Awareness, says:

> No nation at the UN Security Council has been more steadfast or consistent in resistance to U.S. and Western sanctions efforts there than either the bear or the dragon. The reasons for this are quite simple: Synergistic strategic advancement against a common enemy, oil and money. Iran is rightly portrayed as one of the most pressing threats to the United States and her interests. But Iran remains in many respects a piece on the chessboard of a greater Russian and Chinese game. Iran seeks greater power and regional dominance and enjoys the support of both Russia and China in its pursuits. Both afford Iran the protection of cover and interference at the UN Security Council and other

diplomatic endeavors, allowing Iran to continue its nuclear efforts under a fairly comfortable security blanket.

For Russia . . . the gains are monetary and psychological, with Iran as a major arms client . . . China . . . signed a massive long-term energy deal with Iran worth billions. The United States in particular had made . . . public calls for other nations to specifically stop making energy agreements until Iran complies [with UN calls for halting the nuclear program]. Signing the energy deal . . . [afforded] the oil-starved dragon energy relief . . . All seek to weaken the United States to the point where each is enabled to act on their respective interests.[97]

Each of these three nations has a different agenda in seeking relationship with the others in the group: Iran wishes to gain superiority in the Persian Gulf and continue its support for the terrorist groups which act as its proxies; Russia, the once-proud bear desires to regain a dominant role on the world stage; and China, the Johnny-come-lately dragon to the international political scene desires to wrest the "superpower" title from the United States, and desperately needs the oil flowing from Iran. So long as America remains strong politically, economically and militarily, those wishes will be thwarted, but we have too often seen the U.S. falter in all three categories since early 2009.

With the recent easing of sanctions on Iran, it is imperative not to think all is well and relax the vigilance. It might behoove both China and Russia to take notice of an event which took place following the botched elections in Tehran in June 2009. According to a *Miami Herald* report:

> In Tehran University's huge prayer hall, the Islamic regime's most powerful clerics deliver heated Friday sermons to thousands. These diatribes are normally accompanied by the chant "Death to America!"
>
> But at the last Friday prayers [July 17, 2009]—an electrifying event that will affect the core of President

Obama's foreign policy—the loudest chants were

'Death to Russia!" and "Death to China!" Also, "Azadeh!" which means "freedom" in Farsi . . . Consider the impact of this new list of enemies. Ahmadinejad has been trying to distract attention from rigged elections by blaming the West for stirring up demonstrations.[98]

The next issue to be addressed when contemplating the question of how the West can be saved from an apocalyptic event orchestrated by Islamic Infidels is that of globalization. What is it and what effect might it have on saving the West from Iran's nuclear pursuits and apocalyptic mission? Globalization is defined as:

A process of interaction and integration among the people, companies, and governments of different nations, a process driven by international trade and investment and aided by information technology. This process has effects on the environment, on culture, on political systems, on economic development and prosperity, and on human physical well-being in societies around the world.[99]

Globalization knows no borders; it crosses international boundaries. Observe how easily Islamic State jihadists cross borders in the Middle East and in Europe. That is why the fight against terrorism in any form must first be global. No one is exempt from the hatred and fanaticism which grips these radical Islamic Infidels. Having explored the dangers of nuclear weapons in the hands of leaders such as those in power in Tehran, or slipping into the hands of Islamic Infidels in IS ranks, we must define ways in which the world community can halt the forward progress of such fanaticism.

A unified world marketplace would have a major impact on the economy of the Islamic Infidels who wish to foist a caliphate on the world. Global social media tools are used by terrorist groups to plot and carry out strikes, to fundraise, and to attract new members. Those same tools could be used to divulge the names and faces of members, as well as plans for attacks. Globalization could be a vital tool in halting the forward march toward an apocalypse, but only if all world leaders are engaged. It would directly affect markets, economies, communications, transportation, trade, service industries, and capital. It clearly could be a determining factor in whether or not sanctions against Iran were effective. It could be used to leverage Iran's oil-based economy.

In a speech delivered at the National Defense College graduation ceremony in July 2009, Israel's Benjamin Netanyahu addressed the effectiveness of globalization:

> Eventually radical Islam will be defeated by the global information revolution, by the freedom of ideas which are breaking out, through technology and through ideas of freedom. This won't happen immediately, but it will happen . . . *The only thing that can postpone and disrupt the rate of the extinguishing of radical Islam is the possibility that it will be armed with a nuclear weapon.*[100]
> (Emphasis mine)

The Syrians are controlled today by the Islamic State

in the area of the country that housed the nuclear reactor destroyed by Israel. Former Vice President Dick Cheney in his book, *Cheney: One on One,* lauded the Israelis for their move. I will leave you to consider the global impact the capture by Islamic Infidels of a nuclear plant would have.

13

WINNING the WAR THROUGH PRAYER

*There is a big difference between fighting
the cold war and fighting radical Islam.
The rules have changed, and we haven't.*[101]

JOHN LE CARRÉ,
BESTSELLING AUTHOR

THIS QUESTION IS NOW OBVIOUS given the secular and spiritual implications: Can a war against Islamic Infidels be fought and won? To recap, IS was formed as a splinter group of al Qaeda and today numbers upwards of twenty thousand armed Islamic Infidels. The barbarous entity is funded with money from oil fields captured in Iraq and Syria, and occupies large parcels of territory in both countries which includes cities as large as Mosul, Iraq. It is adept in the use of social media for recruitment and to advertise its heinous crimes against humanity. While it is capable of spreading fear and wreaking havoc, it is not in any way remarkable.

In an article for *The New Yorker*, journalist Steve Coll offered this opinion:

> If President Obama ordered the Marines into urgent action, they could be waving flags of liberation in Raqqa by New Year's. But, after taking the region, killing scores of isis commanders as well as Syrian civilians, and flushing surviving fighters and international recruits into the broken, ungoverned cities of Syria and Iraq's Sunni heartland, then what? Without political coöperation from Bashar al-Assad, Russia, Iran, Hezbollah, Iraqi Shiite militias, Turkey, the Al Qaeda ally Al Nusra, Saudi Arabia, the Gulf States, and others, the Marines (and the French or nato allies that might assist them) would soon become targets for a mind-bogglingly diverse array of opponents.[102]

Those in favor of such action might urge that it would be worth the effort and the loss to eradicate the likes of IS and its murderous hordes. Following the slaughter and decimation in Paris and in San Bernardino, less level-headed leaders might call for that option. We should, however, have learned vital lessons from Afghanistan (where the Taliban is enjoying a moderate resurgence) and in Iraq (a country still in a state of turmoil). Such a move would not be a sensible course on which to embark.

With only a short time remaining of his two terms in office, President Obama, who is apparently not a proponent of challenging IS on the ground in Syria and Iraq, will probably remain on the sidelines. It is unlikely that he will taint his "legacy" by doing more than just maintaining the status quo. This inaction will deposit the war against IS into the inbox of the next occupant of the Oval Office.

Islamic Infidels are not confined to roving hordes; they come in all shapes, sizes, and numbers. In 2009, Army Major Nidal Hasan stationed at Fort Hood, Texas, was heard to shout, "Allahu akbar!" as he calmly murdered 13 people and injured more than thirty. It was not the last time that cry has been heard in association with terror attacks worldwide.

Incredibly, the President and his staff labeled this heinous crime "workplace violence." Hasan eventually wrote
to ISIL leaders requesting that he be allowed to join the
Islamic State.

A second such instance occurred in Moore, Oklahoma,
in September 2014. Alton Nobel, a food-plant worker who
had recently converted to Islam, decapitated a fellow
employee in a fit of rage as he, too, allegedly screamed
Islamic expressions. His acts have also unbelievably been
categorized as merely "workplace violence" and not an act
of terrorism. Again I ask: Where is the outrage when U.S.
citizens have been slaughtered by homegrown terrorists
and it is shrugged off as 'workplace violence'? Has our
nation become the frog in the pot of cold water, oblivious
to the fire beneath until it is too late? Did Americans elect
and then reelect a president so complacent that when
the Middle East erupts into flames, we will be forced to
give in without a fight? What prompts such devastating
murder and mayhem? The answer can be found in the
book of Genesis, Chapter 6:8b-9, NKJV:

> It came to pass, when they were
> in the field, that Cain rose up against
> Abel his brother and killed him.

> Then the LORD said to Cain, "Where
> *is* Abel your brother?" He said, "I do
> not know. *Am* I my brother's keeper?"
> (Genesis 4:9, NKJV)

In Genesis 6:5-6, we see a picture of the heart of God when violence became rampant over His creation:

> Then the LORD saw that the wick-
> edness of man *was* great in the earth,
> and *that* every intent of the thoughts
> of his heart *was* only evil continually.
> And the LORD was sorry that He had
> made man on the earth, and He was
> grieved in His heart.

Rabbi Lord Jonathan Sacks in his book, *Not in God's Name: Confronting Religious Violence* wrote:

> When religion turns men into
> murderers, God weeps. So the book of
> Genesis tells us . . . . Too often in the
> history of religion, people have killed
> in the name of the God of life, waged
> war in the name of the God of peace,
> hated in the name of the God of love

and practiced cruelty in the name of the God of compassion. When this happens God speaks, sometimes in a still small voice almost inaudible beneath the clamor of those claiming to speak on his behalf. What he says at such times is: *Not in My name.*[103]

Islam has been hijacked by a band of Islamic Infidels whose weapon of choice is terrorism in all its murderous facets. The world is faced with the question of how to meet and defeat this growing threat. During the Arab Spring in the early days of the first decade of the twenty-first century, several Arab countries attempted to counter the fanatical element with a desire for democracy. Few, if any, of the intolerant and despotic practitioners of Islam appreciate the basic elements of a democratic society: freedom of speech, freedom of the press, the rule of law, and religious tolerance among others. They are unacquainted with the meaning of an open and free election in countries where women were, and are, denied the most basic freedoms. One of the failures of converting to a democracy was the realization that in Western culture anyone or anything is fair game—including the Prophet Muhammad—which resulted in the attack on the magazine, *Charlie Hebdo*, in Paris in January 2017, and the ensuing carnage.[104]

President Obama's politically correct, yet absurd, statement that the Islamic State has nothing to do with Islam tends to make it even more difficult to launch an attack against the enemy that is radical Islam. The United States and Israel have a very identifiable foe—Islamic Infidels. In order to defeat them, we must join with our Western allies and Arab nations to end the threat.

Author and talk-show host Tammy Bruce offered these suggestions for quelling terror attacks in the West by Islamic Infidels. She suggested:

> First, Islamists who go to the Middle East to train and fight with a terrorist army must not be allowed to return to any Western nation.
>
> Second, acknowledge this is a world war and stop treating terrorism . . . with regular civil crime.

Third, imprison the terrorist enemy
in military prisons, ending their ability
to "radicalize" civilians in prison.

Fourth, as in wartime, arrest those
who spread propaganda for the enemy,
recruit for the enemy and support the
enemy.[105]

There is another question that must be asked, and that
is: What would Jesus have us do? Paul wrote in Romans
12:19, NKJV:

Beloved, do not avenge yourselves,
but *rather* give place to wrath; for it
is written, "Vengeance *is* Mine, I will
repay," says the Lord.

And Deuteronomy 32:35, NKJV, reminds us the Lord
says:

Vengeance is mine, And I decree
the punishment of all her enemies:
Their doom is sealed.

It is the Enemy who comes to kill, steal and destroy
(see John 10:10); it is he and his minions who are behind

every reprehensible act of violence perpetrated by Islamic Infidels. In Ephesians 6:12, NKJV, the Apostle Paul defines our adversary:

> For we do not wrestle against flesh and blood, but against principalities, against powers, against the rulers of the darkness of this age . . .

To the church in Corinth, Paul wrote:

> For though we walk in the flesh, we do not war according to the flesh. 4 For the weapons of our warfare *are* not carnal but mighty in God for pulling down strongholds. (2 Corinthians 10:3-4, NKJV)

It was Alfred Lord Tennyson who opined, "More things are wrought by prayer than this world dreams of."[106]

Just as America may be forced to once again take the war on terrorism to the nations that sponsor it, so must we who bear the name of Christ take our fight to the battlefield in the spiritual realm. We must take the battle to the enemy and defeat it through prayer in the name of Jesus!

Prayer is the only exploit that takes hold of eternity. It is the action that touches Heaven. It pierces the heart of God, turns the head of God, and moves the hand of God. For a Christian, it is not the last resort . . . it is the first resort!

Through prayer, we must do everything possible to overthrow kingdoms of darkness, shut the mouths of the lions of terror, and quench the flames of Hell by the power of Almighty God! How you and I respond to God's call will determine whether we succeed or fail.

ENDNOTES

1. Bruce J. Evenson, *Truman, Palestine and the Cold War*, www.jstor.org/stable/4283481, p.131,; accessed February 2016.

2. http://www.jpost.com/Middle-East/ISIS-Threat/The-only-country-ISIS-fears-in-the-Middle-East-is-Israel-438576; accessed January 2016.

3. Amotz Asa-el, "The drop in oil prices is ISIS's first strategic defeat," Market Watch, http://www.marketwatch.com/story/the-drop-in-oil-prices-is-isiss-first-strategic-defeat-2014-10-16; accessed February 2016.

4. Alexandra Douglas, "Central Intelligence Agency chief: ISIS used chemical weapons, may have more," http://quadrangleonline.com/2016/02/13/central-intelligence-agency-chief-isis-used-chemical/; accessed January 2016.

5. Graeme Wood, "What ISIS Really Wants," *The Atlantic*, http://www.theatlantic.com/magazine/archive/2015/03/what-isis-really-wants/384980/; accessed February 2016.

6. David Ignatius, "How ISIS Spread in the Middle East And How to Stop it," The Atlantic, October 29, 2015; http://belfercenter.ksg.harvard.edu/publication/25952/how_isis_spread_in_the_middle_east.html; accessed January 2016.

7. Definition of apocalyptism, http://www.bing.com/search?q=+apocalyptism&form=PRUSEN&pc=U348&mkt=en-us&refig=354623c1714549768d99fe9b85f25545; accessed January 2016.

8. http://www.dailymail.co.uk/news/article-2786039/The-1-300-year-old-apocalyptic-prophecy-predicted-war-Islamic-army-infidel-horde-Syria-fuelling-ISIS-s-brutal-killers.html#ixzz40R9vGwl9; accessed January 2016.

9. Robert Spencer, "Islamic State: "We will conquer your Rome, break your crosses, and enslave your women, by the permission of Allah," http://www.jihadwatch.org/2014/09/islamic-state-we-will-conquer-your-rome-break-your-crosses-and-enslave-your-women-by-the-permission-of-allah; accessed February 2016.

10. Nick Butler, "ISIS and the war for oil," http://blogs.ft.com/nick-butler/2016/01/10/isis-and-the-war-for-oil/; accessed February 2016.

11. "ISIS, facing cash shortage, cuts back on perks and salaries," Fox News, February 16, 2016, http://www.foxnews.com/world/2016/02/16/isis-facing-cash-shortage-cuts-back-on-perks-and-salaries.html; accessed February 2016.

12. https://en.wikipedia.org/wiki/Infidel; accessed January 2016.

13. George W. Bush, White House Archives, http://georgewbush-whitehouse. archives.gov/news/releases/2001/09/20010917-11.html; accessed January 2016.

14. Sahar Aziz: Identifying the Wrong Culprit for Terrorism, *The Dallas Morning News,* November 25, 2015, http://www.dallasnews.com/opinion/ latest-columns/20151124-sahar-aziz-identifying-the-wrong-culprit-for-terrorism.ece; accessed January 2016.

15. Terrorism: Muslim Brotherhood, Jewish Virtual Library, https://www. jewishvirtuallibrary.org/jsource/Terrorism/muslimbrotherhood.html; accessed January 2016.

16. Islam 101; http://www.islam101.com/dawah/pillars.html, accessed June 2009.

17. Hamza Hendawi, "Islamic State's double standards sow growing disillusion," http://www.msn.com/en-us/news/world/islamic-states-double-standards-sow-growing-disillusion/ar-BBonCK1?li=BBnbcA1&ocid= U348DHP; accessed January 2016.

18. http://www.cbc.ca/news/politics/daesh-adopted-as-new-name-for-isis-by-u-s-france-1.2861108; accessed January 2016.

19. Bob Dylan, "Gotta Serve Somebody," http://www.bobdylan.com/us/songs/ gotta-serve-somebody; accessed January 2016.

20. Mike Evans, "Not Radical Islamists, but Islamic Infidels," The Jerusalem Post, http://www.jpost.com/Opinion/Not-radical-Islamists-but-Islamic-infidels-439257; accessed December 2016.

21. http://www.apologeticsindex.org/s41.html; accessed January 2016.

22. "What is Salafism and Should We Be Worried About it?" January 19, 2015, http://www.theweek.co.uk/world-news/6073/what-is-salafism-and-should-we-be-worried-by-it; accessed January 2016.

23. Muhammad Munir, "Suicide Attacks and Islamic Law," https://www.icrc. org/eng/assets/files/other/irrc-869_munir.pdf; accessed January 2016.

24. "Ayman al-Zawahiri," http://www.jewishvirtuallibrary.org/jsource/ biography/Zawahiri.html; accessed January 2016.

25. "Hearing Before the Sub-committee on Terrorism, Technology and Homeland Security of the Committee on the Judiciary, United States Senate, 108th Congress, First Session, June 26, 2003, Serial No. J–108–21; accessed January 2016; accessed January 2016.

26. Alexander H. Joffe, "ISIS and Antiquities: The Missing Pieces," January 25, 2016, http://www.meforum.org/5809/isis-antiquities; accessed February 2016.

27. Steve Coll, "Letter from Jedda: Young Osama, (How He Learned Radicalism and May Have Seen America)" *The New Yorker*, December 12, 2005, http://www.mafhoum.com/press9/259C37.htm; accessed January 2016.

28. "Obama is wrong: Islamic beliefs are incompatible with the modern world," February 21, 2015, http://scholarsandrogues.com/2015/02/21/obama-is-wrong-islamic-beliefs-are-incompatible-with-the-modern-world/; accessed January 2016.

29. Mansour al-Nogaidan, "Losing my Jihadism," *Washington Post*, July 22, 2007, http://www.washingtonpost.com/wp-dyn/content/article/2007/07/20/AR2007072001808.html; accessed January 2016.

30. Neil MacFarquhar, "A Nation Challenged: Education; Anti-Western and Extremist Views Pervade Saudi Schools", *The New York Times*, October 19, 2001, http://www.nytimes.com/2001/10/19/world/nation-challenged-education-anti-western-extremist-views-pervade-saudi-schools. html?pagewanted=1; accessed January 2016.

31. http://www.pbs.org/wgbh/pages/frontline/shows/saudi/analyses/madrassas.html; accessed January 2016.

32. Ibid

33. Ibid

34. Soren Kern, "Salafism in Germany: Something Must be Done Immediately," http://www.gatestoneinstitute.org/4342/germany-salafism; accessed January 2016.

35. David Brooks, "War of Ideology," *The New York Times*, July 24, 2004, http://www.nytimes.com/2004/07/24/opinion/war-of-ideology.html; accessed January 2016.

36. Roger Scruton, *The West and the Rest: Globalization and the Terrorist Threat* (Wilmington, DE: ISI Books, 2002), 91.

37. Lucy S. Davidowicz, *The War Against the Jews 1933-1945* (Bantam Books, New York, NY 1986), 8-9.

38. Karl Dietrich Bracher, *The German Dictatorship: The Origins, Structure, and Effects of National Socialism*. Translated by Jean Steinberg, (Holt Rinehart and Winston, New York, NY 1979.) Originally Published under the title *Die Deutsche Diktatur: Entstehung, Struktur, Folgen des Nationalsocialismus*. (Verlag Kiepenheuer & Witsch. Koln and Berlin, 1969), 93

39. Richard J. Evans, *The Coming of the Third Reich* (Penguin Books, New York 2004), 197.

40. Richard Rhodes, *Masters of Death: The SS Einsatzgruppen and the Invention of the Holocaust,* (Vintage Books, a division of Random House, New York, NY 2002), 37.

41. http://www.freerepublic.com/focus/f-news/1369994/posts; accessed January 2016.

42. Russ Read, "The Ideological War with Islamofascism," August 30, 2014, http://www.theblaze.com/contributions/the-ideological-war-with-islamofascism/; accessed January 2016.

43. http://www.presentationmagazine.com/winston-churchill-speech-we-shall-fight-them-on-the-beaches-8003.htm; accessed January 2016.

44. Eugene Kiely, "Obama Fumbles 'JV Team' Question," The Wire, September 8, 2014, http://www.factcheck.org/2014/09/obama-fumbles-jv-team-question/; accessed January 2016.

45. Constitutional attorney John Whitehead, "Terrorism and the Media: A Symbiotic Relationship," http://www.crossroad.to/articles2/0013/whitehead/4-terrorism_media.htm; accessed January 2016.

46. http://www.mediaite.com/online/limbaugh-boyhood-pictures-of-tsarnaev-show-media-trying-to-do-to-him-what-they-did-to-trayvon/; accessed January 2016.

47. Council on Foreign Relations, "Terrorists and the Internet," http://www.cfr.org/terrorism-and-technology/terrorists-internet/p10005; accessed January 2016.

48. "Terrorist Activities on the Internet, Anti-Defamation League," http://archive.adl.org/terror/focus/16_focus_a2.html; accessed January 2016.

49. (http://www.globalsecurity.org/military/library/report/1989/GSM.htm) Dorothy Denning. "Activism, Hacktivism, and Cyberterrorism: The Internet as a Tool for Influencing Foreign Policy." Networks and Netwars: The Future of Terror, Crime and Militancy. Ed. John Arquilla and David Ronfeldt. Santa Monica: RAND, 2001. 239-288; accessed January 2016.

50. Ben Brumfield, "Officials: 3 Denver girls played hooky from school and tried to join ISIS," October 22, 2014, http://www.cnn.com/2014/10/22/us/colorado-teens-syria-odyssey/index.html; accessed January 2016.

51. As quoted in—Terrorism—How the West Can Win. Awake! magazine, 1/8—1987, https://en.wikiquote.org/wiki/Terrorism; accessed January 2016.

52. Bridget Gabriel, Because They Hate (New York, NY: St. Martin's Press:2006), 145.

53. Ronald Reagan, "A Time for Choosing," October 27, 1964, http://www.nationalcenter.org/ReaganChoosing1964.html; accessed January 2016.

54. Winston Churchill, "Their Finest Hour," http://www.historyplace.com/speeches/churchill-hour.htm; accessed January 2016.

55. Bruce Walker, "Why They Hate us, September 18, 2012, "http://www.americanthinker.com/2012/09/why_they_hate_ us.html#ixzz3x9BLmaaLaccessed January 2016.

56. Gabriel, 156-157.

57. http://www.zionism-israel.com/log/archives/00000068.html; accessed January 2016.

58. Paul Alster, "Gruesome photos may show ISIS using chemical weapons on Kurds, report says," October 13, 2014, http://www.foxnews.com/ world/2014/10/13/gruesome-photos-may-show-isis-using-chemical- weapons-on-kurds-says-report/; accessed October 2014.

59. Arthur Ahlert, "Saddam's WMDs: The Left's Iraq Lies Exposed," June 23, 2014, http://www.frontpagemag.com/2014/arnold-ahlert/saddams-wmds- the-lefts-iraq-lies-exposed/; accesses October 2014.

60. Martin Luther King, Jr. (1929-68), U.S. clergyman, civil rights leader. Strength to Love, Philadelphia, Fortress Press, pt. 4, ch. 3 (1963).

61. http://www.bing.com/search?q=+Savielly+Tartakower&form=PRUSEN&pc =U348&mkt=en-us&refig=ab6e710a7d8944c396322f9b58262824&pq=savie lly+tartakower&sc=2-19&sp=-1&qs=n&sk=&cvid=ab6e710a7d8944c396322f 9b58262824; accessed January 2016.

62. Louis Rene Beres and Tsiddon-Chatto, Col. (res.) Yoash, "Reconsidering Israel's Destruction of Iraq's Osiraq Nuclear Reactor," *Temple International and Comparative Law Journal 9 (2)*, 1995. Reprinted in *Israel's Strike Against the Iraqi Nuclear Reactor 7 June 1982*, Jerusalem: Menachem Begin Heritage Center, 2003, p.60.

63. On *GlobalSecurity.org*. This Internet site contains an extensive discussion of Iran's nuclear facilities, including a site-by-site description, reached by navigating through the following sequence: Iran > Facilities > Nuclear. The discussion of Iran's uranium mines is drawn from this site: http://www. globalsecurity.org/wmd/world/iran/mines.htm. (Accessed 2006)

64. Nasser Karimi, "Iran Official Denies Report of Nuclear Reactor Being Sealed," January 12, 2016, ABC News, http://abcnews.go.com/International/ wireStory/iran-official-denies-report-nuclear-reactor-sealed-36230678; accessed January 2016.

65. Ibid

66. Reza Kahlili, "Ayatollah: Kill all Jews, Annihilate Israel," *World Net Daily*, February 5, 2012, http://www.wnd.com/2012/02/ayatollah-kill-all-jews- annihilate-israel/#dUomRSFSddGwcqWP.99; accessed November 2013.

67. Josep Federman, "Netanyahu: Iran Nuclear Deal a 'historic mistake'," *Huffington Post*, November 25, 2013, http://www.huffingtonpost. com/2013/11/24/netanyahu-iran-deal-israel-nuclear_n_4332906.html; accessed November 2013.

68. "Arabs not allied with Iran not quiet over nuclear deal," *USAToday*, November 24, 2013, http://www.usatoday.com/story/news/ world/2013/11/24/iran-nuclear-deal-arab-reactions/3691289/; accessed November 2013.

69. Lewis Carroll, *Alice's Adventures in Wonderland & Through the Looking-Glass,* http://www.goodreads.com/quotes/tag/chess; accessed January 2016.

70. Council on Foreign Relations; State Sponsors: Iran; August 2007, http:// www.cfr.org/publication/9362/#5. (Accessed February 2008.)

71. "Proxy Power: Understanding Iran's use of Terrorists"; Brookings Institution; http://brookings.edu/opinoins/2006/0726iran_byman.aspx. (Accessed February 2008.)

72. "Iran, Hizbullah, Hamas and the Global Jihad: A New Conflict Paradigm for the West" 2007; Gen. (Ret.) Moshe Ya'alon, "The Second Lebanon War: From Territory to Ideology", Jerusalem Center for Public Affairs; p. 16. (Accessed January 2008.)

73. Iran Terror: List of Terror Attacks, July 19, 2005. (http://www.iranterror. com/content/view/38/56/. (Accessed February 2008.)

74. *The 9/11 Commission Report*, Chapter 7, Section 3 (Washington: U. S. Government Printing Office, 2004) p. 240.

75. Susanne Knaul, "Hope Mixed with Apprehension," *The Atlantic Times*, April 15, 2011; www.the-atlantic-times.com/index.php?option=com_ content&view=article&id=372. Accessed April 2011.

76. http://www.cfr.org/israel/palestinian-islamic-jihad/p15984; accessed January 2016.

77. http://www.jewishvirtuallibrary.org/jsource/Terrorism/PIJ.html; accessed January 2016.

78. Prime Minister Benjamin Netanyahu, http://www.imra.org.il/story. php3?id=65006; accessed September 2014.

79. http://www.express.co.uk/news/world/612425/Islamic-State-ISIS-Assyrian-Christians-caliphate-Gothenburg-Sweden-jihadis; accessed January 2016.

80. http://news.yahoo.com/the-doomsday-ideology-of-isis-192945938.html; accessed January 2016.

81. http://teachinghistory.org/history-content/ask-a-historian/24468; accessed December 2015.

82. http://finance.yahoo.com/news/major-world-event-syrian-war-134900535. html; accessed October 2015.

83. http://www.telegraph.co.uk/news/worldnews/europe/russia/11903702/ Russias-Vladimir-Putin-launches-strikes-in-Syria-on-Isil-to-US-anger-live-updates.html; accessed October 2015.

84. Neil MacFarquhar, Questions Linger over Russia's Endgame in Syria, Ukraine and Europe, The New York Times, February 23, 2016; http://www. nytimes.com/2016/02/24/world/europe/russia-endgame-syria-ukraine-europe.html, accessed February 2016.

85. http://www.reuters.com/article/2015/10/02/us-mideast-crisis-syria-airstrikes-idUSKCN0RW0W220151002; accessed October 2015.

86. CNN, September 11, 2014, http://www.cnn.com/2014/09/10/politics/obama-isil-not-islamic/index.html; accessed August 2015.

87. John Dryden, "A Song for St. Cecelia's Day," http://www.notable-quotes. com/a/apocalypse_quotes_iii.html#0hhojGAL.b7db5OOF.99; accessed January 2016.

88. Voltaire, *The Philosophical Dictionary*, Kindle edition, downloadable at http://www.gutenberg.org/ebooks/18569, location 1,030.

89. http://christinprophecy.org/articles/the-interpretation-of-the-book/; accessed September 2015.

90. In fact, if you search for "Persepolis" in Google Earth, it will take you to the site of this celebration. In the satellite image, you can still see the five-pointed star of roadways for the pavilions built for the guests of this event.

91. See my book, *The Final Move Beyond Iraq*, for more on this.

92. For more on "Fumbling Iran," see the chapter with that title in my book, *The Final Move Beyond Iraq*.

93. For a quick study of this history, you can get a cursory understanding from the 1966 film *Khartoum*, or one of the various remakes of the film, like *The Four Feathers*, that use the rise of Sudan's Mahdi as a backdrop.

94. Hillary Leila Krieger, "Turkey has embraced the leaders of Iran and HAMAS," *The Jerusalem Post*, June 6, 2011; http://www.jpost.com/ International/Article.aspx?id=177577; accessed July 14, 2015.

95. Jeremy Diamond, "Dick Cheney warns of potential 9/11 with 'much deadlier weapons'," http://www.cnn.com/2015/08/31/politics/dick-cheney-terrorism-threat-isis/index.html; accessed September 2015.

96. In the *King James Bible*, this phrase is translated as *"the merchants of Tarshish, with all the young lions thereof,"* which throws a different light on the passage, though no clearer. Some suggest again that *"the young lions"* refer to the colonies of Europe [BRITAIN - BECAUSE ITS EMBLEM WAS THE LION?], or perhaps a military group such as NATO.

97. Jamie Glazov, "The China-Russia-Iran Axis", *FrontPageMagazine.com*, January 22, 2008, http://www.frontpagemag.com/readArticle.aspx?ARTID=29604; accessed August 2015.

98. Trudy Rubin, "Hold Off Engaging Iran," *Miami Herald*, July 23, 2009; http://www.miamiherald.com/opinion/other-views/v-fullstory/story/1153627.html; accessed August 2015.

99. "What is Globalization?" http://www.globalization101.org/What_is_Globalization.html?PHPSESSID=e54636b5a846c31e34b20315060d2a71; accessed August 2015.

100. Benjamin Netanyahu, Translation, Prime Minister's Office, July 28, 2009; http://www.pmo.gov.il/PMOEng/Communication/PMSpeaks/speechmabal280709.htm; accessed August 2015.

101. http://www.azquotes.com/quotes/topics/radical-islam.html; accessed January 2016.

102. Steve Coll, "ISIS After Paris," *The New Yorker*, November 30, 2015, http://www.newyorker.com/magazine/2015/11/30/isis-after-paris; accessed January 2016.

103. Rabbi Lord Jonathan Sacks, *Not in My Name: Confronting Religious Violence* (New York City: Schocken Books, a division of Penguin Random House, 2015), 3.

104. http://www.bbc.com/news/world-europe-30708237; accessed January 2016.

105. Tammy Bruce, "Four lessons from Paris attacks: What must happen now to stop radical Islam," http://www.foxnews.com/opinion/2015/01/12/four-lessons-from-paris-attacks-what-must-happen-now-to-stop-radical-islam.html; accessed January 2016.

106. http://www.goodreads.com/quotes/147923-more-things-are-wrought-by-prayer-than-this-world-dreams; accessed January 2016.

MICHAEL DAVID EVANS, the #1 *New York Times* bestselling author, is an award-winning journalist/Middle East analyst. Dr. Evans has appeared on hundreds of network television and radio shows including *Good Morning America*, *Crossfire* and *Nightline*, and *The Rush Limbaugh Show*, and on Fox Network, *CNN World News*, NBC, ABC, and CBS. His articles have been published in the *Wall Street Journal*, *USA Today*, *Washington Times*, *Jerusalem Post* and newspapers worldwide. More than twenty-five million copies of his books are in print, and he is the award-winning producer of nine documentaries based on his books.

Dr. Evans is considered one of the world's leading experts on Israel and the Middle East, and is one of the most sought-after speakers on that subject. He is the chairman of the board of the Ten Boom Holocaust Museum in Haarlem, Holland, and is the founder of Israel's first Christian museum—Friends of Zion: Heroes and History—in Jerusalem.

Dr. Evans has authored a number of books including: *History of Christian Zionism*, *Showdown with Nuclear Iran*, *Atomic Iran*, *The Next Move Beyond Iraq*, *The Final Move Beyond Iraq*, and *Countdown*. His body of work also includes the novels *Seven Days*, *GameChanger*, *The Samson Option*, *The Four Horsemen*, *The Locket*, *Born Again: 1967*, and *The Columbus Code*.

✦ ✦ ✦

Michael David Evans is available to speak or for interviews. Contact: EVENTS@drmichaeldevans.com.

BOOKS BY: MIKE EVANS

Israel: America's Key to Survival

Save Jerusalem

The Return

Jerusalem D.C.

Purity and Peace of Mind

Who Cries for the Hurting?

Living Fear Free

I Shall Not Want

Let My People Go

Jerusalem Betrayed

Seven Years of Shaking: A Vision

The Nuclear Bomb of Islam

Jerusalem Prophecies

Pray For Peace of Jerusalem

America's War:
The Beginning of the End

The Jerusalem Scroll

The Prayer of David

The Unanswered Prayers of Jesus

God Wrestling

The American Prophecies

Beyond Iraq: The Next Move

The Final Move beyond Iraq

Showdown with Nuclear Iran

Jimmy Carter: The Liberal Left
and World Chaos

Atomic Iran

Cursed

Betrayed

The Light

Corrie's Reflections & Meditations

The Revolution

The Final Generation

Seven Days

The Locket

GAMECHANGER SERIES:

GameChanger

Samson Option

The Four Horsemen

THE PROTOCOLS SERIES:

The Protocols

The Candidate

Persia: The Final Jihad

Jerusalem

The History of Christian Zionism

Countdown

Ten Boom: Betsie, Promise of God

Commanded Blessing

Born Again: 1948

Born Again: 1967

Presidents in Prophecy

Stand with Israel

Prayer, Power and Purpose

Turning Your Pain Into Gain

Christopher Columbus, Secret Jew

Living in the F.O.G.

Finding Favor with God

Finding Favor with Man

Unleashing God's Favor

The Jewish State: The Volunteers

See You in New York

Friends of Zion: Patterson & Wingate

The Columbus Code

The Temple

Satan, You Can't Have My Country!

Satan, You Can't Have Israel!

COMING SOON:

Netanyahu

Lights in the Darkness

TO PURCHASE, CONTACT: orders@timeworthybooks.
com P. O. BOX 30000, PHOENIX, AZ 85046